Woman to Woman

Winning at Work

Career Success Secrets for Women in the Workplace

AMBER KAMPS

Woman to Woman
Winning at Work, Career Success Secrets for Women in the Workplace

Amber Kamps

Published By:
Woman To Woman Solutions

www.WomanToWomanSolutions.com

The opinions, views, advice and stories in this book are those of the author and in no way reflect the views of the employers the author has worked for in the past.

ISBN-13: 978-1535141451

DEDICATION

This book is dedicated to all the women who make this world go round. It is my sincere hope this book makes a difference in both your personal and professional life.

JUST FOR YOU!

This book will change you. It will change how you think, how you act, and how you choose to live your life from this day forward. And as such, I wanted to give you something as an extra bonus so you could make the most out of this book and the ideas, strategies, and secrets provided.

I have created a free downloadable workbook just for you which seeks to compliment and enhance your reading experience of this book. This workbook follows each chapter in order and includes bonus material such as highlighting key points, questions and ideas to think or write about in your journal, diving deeper exercises, and more. Please visit the following website to download your free copy:

www.WomanToWomanSolutions.com/workbook

CONTENTS

1 Introduction 1

2 The Playing Field Is Our Reality 7

3 The Secret to It All 12

4 Purposeful Consciousness 22

5 Yes, It's a Man's World 27

6 How to Be Taken Seriously, Despite Being a Female in a Man's World 32

7 Too Aggressive or Bossy? Thanks for the Compliment 42

8 Not Getting the Same Opportunities as Your Male Counterparts? Create Your Own 46

9 The Oppressive Atmosphere Makes Me Feel Like There Is No Respect for My Opinion or Contribution 49

10 Don't Make Me Choose & Then Punish Me for My Choice 63

11 It's Exhausting Having to Prove Myself Over & Over Again 69

12 Not Listened to, Not Understood, or Talked Over 74

13 Tears at Work Suck 80

14 Being Female Means I'm Not Smart Enough or Strong Enough? Give Me a Break! 85

15 I'm Tired of Being Called the Diversity Hire! 91

16 Women Can't Be Good Managers Because They Are   95
Too Emotional

17 I'm Convinced If I Start a Family, My Career Will End   100

18 Work-life Balance: Is it a Dream or Is It a Nightmare?   106

19 Bullying & Sexual Harassment Is a Big Deal   113

20 When It's the Women in the Workplace Who Are a   119
Problem

21 Failure Is Not the Final Frontier   131

22 Conclusion & Final Thoughts   139

1

INTRODUCTION

It was a very hot August afternoon, the kind of day where sweat pours down your face even when you're standing still. I was at work when I suddenly found myself toe-to-toe in a confrontation. I had taken a new position as a district manager four months prior and I was now at the height of fire season with a 30,000-acre forest fire in the district I was responsible for. The confrontation was with a man, the incident commander, who was sent to my district to manage this fire with his team of hand-picked specialists.

The incident commander had made a decision earlier in the day to proceed with his own plans in fighting the fire that were in direct conflict with what he had been instructed to do when he arrived. He had marched bulldozers up a ridge to build a sixteen-foot-wide fire line in an area managed for the public as roadless. Needless to say, I was angry. I wasn't sure what I was angrier about, the resource damage he'd created or that he had ignored clear direction he had been given. I had no other choice than to meet with him to discuss the situation.

I walked into his camp and told him we needed to talk, which immediately made him angry. He began talking loudly about it not being a good time as he worked his way into my personal space. He stood quite a bit taller and was literally speaking down to me about how I didn't know what I was doing or what I wanted. He also told me I needed to do what he told me to do, rather than the other way around. His posture and body language were purposely intimidating as he stood mere inches from my face. Because two of his team members were standing right behind him, he was definitely trying to show them he was top dog in this situation. I was in a slight state of shock—I couldn't believe that this was actually happening. My heart was beating so fast, and I'm certain my face was flushed. The intense feeling of fight or flight washed over me. Quickly, I snapped into reality when he ended his long-winded slam to my intelligence by saying, "So don't get your panties in a wad!" And if that wasn't bad enough. he added, "Shouldn't you be home taking care of your babies anyway?"

My experience in fire management and working with teams like his was not new. I started fighting fire in 1988, a few weeks after turning eighteen, and I loved it. Yes, this man had more experience than I, but he had no right or reason to berate me the way he did. It didn't help that his team members standing behind him smiled and laughed at his comments. And yes, I had a nine-month-old baby and a two-year-old at home.

I didn't move from my position and stayed toe-to-toe with the man and said, in the most confident voice I could muster, "I don't wear panties, I wear a thong and there isn't much there to make into a wad."

I have no idea where those words came from, but they did the trick. He took three steps back. He was speechless and so were his buddies. Obviously being a mother had nothing to do with this situation, so I didn't justify his comment to being home with my babies with a response of any kind.

This gave me the opening to sternly and professionally remind him that he worked for me, and he and his team would not be allowed to talk to me in this manner from this point forward. I continued to give them clear direction and explained what I expected from them, which included halting the dozer line construction and completing full rehabilitation of it. When I was done I asked if they had any questions. They did not and excused themselves to begin working on my requests.

* * * * *

In my experience, there are not many women in the working world who know how to handle these types of situations. When I was younger, I wouldn't have either, but by that point I'd had many life experiences that helped me get to a place where I had the confidence to speak up and take charge. More women, or, dare I say, all women need the skills and confidence to be successful in dealing with workplace issues and conflict.

My entire career has been about supervising and leading people, particularly young people as they enter the workforce and begin their quest in climbing the ladder. In my experience, the number of young women who have a grasp on navigating the workforce to their benefit is substantially low.

Being a successful woman in the workplace is something I have been asked about my entire career as others saw me achieving success. At first this was a revelation, especially when I started getting invitations to give presentations on "Keys to Success" or "How to Create Work-Life Balance." Me? What did I know? Well, apparently I knew something because as I paid more attention, I realized both men and women in my organization held me in high regard. I personified what a successful woman with a career looked and was still able to balance my roles as a wife and mother.

And furthermore, both men and women would come to me

seeking advice. In one position I held, the workforce made me a sign that read, "The Doctor Is In." What was I doing that was so different from others? I too had fears and lacked confidence just like everyone else. Yet I was doing this differently, some of which was a conscious effort and some of which I have learned about myself over the years.

I do not have a doctorate on the subject of gender inequality, but I do have years in the working world with real life experiences, lessons, tricks, trades, hard truths to share, and maybe even some secrets.

I have worked in natural resource management (forestry, fire suppression, minerals, rangeland, recreation, etc.) for over twenty-five years. I started out as a field-going technician and firefighter. After completing a bachelor's and master's degree, I took positions as a field forester, planning forester, and a specialized forester. Then, for almost twelve years, I held the position of a district manager where I was in charge of 340,000 acres of land and had a staff of over twenty full-time employees and another twenty temporary employees. After needing a break from the demanding and stressful job as a district manager, I took a regional program leadership position working with management at all levels across five states.

As a woman who did successfully move up the ladder as well as a respected manager/decision maker in the organization and community, I set an example to others. I knew this and, although not perfect, I worked hard at being the woman I wanted to be. More days than not I was proud of how I balanced work, employees, kids, husband, health, and community. I actually woke up each morning expecting to "have it all" as I felt I truly did most of the time—I was the district manager I wanted to be, the wife I wanted to be, the mother I wanted to be, and the person I wanted to be. Now I want to share with you what I've learned and how I did it.

* * * * *

I feel so strongly women should support each other in life, but particularly in the workplace. This is especially the case for those women who work in organizations largely dominated by men or organizations with a culture that is not current. As such, I can't think of a better way to share what I have learned and support other women than by writing this book.

In addition to supporting other women, another motivator for me is my son and daughter. This book has much to offer to both men and women, but I truly wrote it for women. The female in my life that most influences me is my teenage daughter.

My kids, from the time they were born, created a new meaning for me in how I chose to live my life and make the choices I do. But it was in having a daughter that my role as a mother took on an additional level of commitment. This commitment was in making sure I was setting the best example of what being a woman looks like. I realize now that this is just as important for my son too, but it wasn't until having a daughter that this light bulb turned on for me.

I believe raising a son is challenging; I believe raising a daughter is more challenging. There are so many more obstacles for females to overcome in this world of ours.

Fortunately for my husband and I, our daughter came out on day one full of spirit and confidence. I will never forget my mother, minutes after my daughter was born, saying she saw something in those girl's eyes that spoke volumes. And to this day, my mother was right. Yet our daughter is facing challenges that work against her spirit and confidence. It breaks my heart that she has been told she is bossy by one of her teachers, she is bullied by older girls in school, and she has to stand up for herself when she isn't treated fairly in all types of situations.

This book is for my daughter and all the other young people just like her as they navigate through life and determine who their authentic self is, build their self-esteem, and learn how to handle conflict.

This book is for all the women out there, regardless of age, as they work in every stage of their careers. This book and the advice in it can help women keep from wasting their valuable time and energy, limiting their talents and assets, and holding back on their futures because they aren't using their strengths and abilities toward positive ends and goals. I don't want to see women limiting themselves because of their gender or because of their age. I don't wish to see women getting trampled on or taking a back seat when they shouldn't. Women have the answers and abilities already inside, but just need the confidence and tools to manifest them. This is why I wrote this book.

* * * * *

Being human is hard. Being a woman is hard. Being a woman in the workforce is harder yet. Women in the workplace face challenges that their male counterparts don't. That is a given.

In life we can't focus on what is fair or what is right, we must determine how to deal with what is.

When life is hard, when bad things happen, or when luck is not on our side, we have to reach inward for strength to get through it. My goal would be for you to be able to reach inward during conflict knowing you can stay true to yourself. I want your playing field to be one where you are prepared to deal with "what is" in a manner where you feel like you are succeeding, achieving, and even winning.

2

THE PLAYING FIELD IS OUR REALITY

In my twenty-five years in the workforce and in my many conversations with other women who work in various fields and companies, there are common issues we have all faced at some point (or many times over) in our working lives. It doesn't matter if you are entering the workforce as a teenager waiting tables, a seasoned middle manager, or a senior-level executive; you are going to face these issues.

Again, this isn't a book about why it is women face these issues. And this isn't a book about how fair it is or isn't. There are many good books and articles on these topics and they are great to read. The "why" of these gender inequalities is important to understand and learn about. However, it's not going to solve your day-to-day problems at work.

For now, this is our reality as women. It's the lay of the land. It's the landscape we must learn to navigate through.

I accept it is our reality, yet I don't accept that it can't change or that it shouldn't change. This is especially true as I think about the women coming in behind me.

However, I believe change can only come by preparing women to successfully deal with the issues they are going to face. I also believe this change can only come by supporting one another as we navigate the tough waters we all know we are going to face.

If we give tools and solutions to women to use and be successful, we will build a new foundation for women to launch from. The grand scheme in all this is to change the culture and the status quo.

My one caveat to you in reading this is that I don't hold all the answers and not everything I share with you will solve all your issues at work. I have failed many, many times in my attempts to prevent issues from occurring and/or in resolving them. I'm the first to admit that I am not perfect and could have done better on many occasions. But I have succeeded too. And in all my trials and errors, I've learned a lot that can be passed on or shared with others. If nothing else, the ideas and stories I will share with you can generate in you a feeling of being supported. Best of all, these may trigger your own tailor-made solutions as you work through your own specific issues.

This book and my words are not to suggest you play games with people, hurt people, undermine people, jeopardize their career, etc. My goal is to share with you productive, positive, and professional means to work through problems at work. There are no "mean girl" approaches in this book. I want you to be effective and successful and to do so in a manner that is above board so you can be proud of how you got to where you are. I want you to be able to look back and know you did your absolute best to support others. Granted we all make mistakes, wish we'd done things differently to achieve a better outcome, say things we shouldn't, or act in ways we regret. But overall, I want you to know in your heart you didn't lie, cheat, or bury someone just to achieve your goals.

* * * * *

Take a look at the following, which are the most common issues women face in the workplace according to my experience and the experience of the women I have had the pleasure of visiting with. I've turned this list of issues into a quiz—see how many of these you have actually faced yourself and/or ring true in your experience. If you answer yes to any or all of these questions, this book is definitely for you.

Most Common Issues Quiz

1. Do you feel you are not taken seriously at work because you are a female?
2. Have you ever been told you are too aggressive or bossy while in a leadership role?
3. Do you feel as if you are not given the same opportunities as your male counterparts?
4. Do you feel oppressed by a manager or supervisor?
5. Have you had to choose between family and work, and when you chose family you suddenly found yourself at the bottom of the heap?
6. Do you feel you have to prove yourself over and over again?
7. Do you feel talked down to because you are a female?
8. Do you struggle to be listened to or understood at work?
9. Do you find you receive little to no respect for your opinion and/or contribution because of your gender?
10. Have you cried at work and/or been ridiculed because of it?
11. Do you find male managers assume you are not smart enough or not tough enough to do some jobs in the organization?

12. Do you feel scrutinized or criticized because you are told you are the "diversity hire?"

13. Have you ever been told women are too emotional and can't be a good manager?

14. Have you ever had a failure you can't seem to overcome?

15. Have you been told you are a distraction due to the size of your chest, the clothes that you wear, or how you smell?

16. Have you ever felt sexually harassed at work?

* * * * *

After reading through the quiz and thinking about your situation, you are likely feeling negative, angry, disheartened, unsettled, or other such feelings. You may even feel like there is no hope as the landscape we women are expected to carry forward in is too hard and unfair. I understand, and I too still feel this way at times.

I think there is great value in knowing what your playing field looks like before you walk into the game. Shouldn't women be in a position where they know and understand how to deal with these issues ahead of time? We as women should be proactive rather than reactive, which would mean being that much further ahead. What would it be like for women to have a strategy in place before they take a new job or enter the workforce? Wouldn't that be a game changer for women in achieving success and in preventing issues from ever surfacing? Wouldn't that be a game changer for our culture as conscious/unconscious bias or tactics just wouldn't work anymore? Women should have both an offense and defense lined up from the start. Isn't this idea empowering? Now we are getting somewhere.

I have read that our society, given the rate of change thus far, is still a hundred years away from gender equality in the workplace. I'm not sure about you, but I'm not willing to wait around that long. The only way I know how to change the gender inequality issues in the workplace are to empower women with the knowledge, tools, and solutions they need to succeed.

When we empower women to handle gender inequality situations and teach them how to prevent them or be proactive, we can then create meaningful and lasting change.

I am in no way suggesting men don't need to change and our current culture doesn't need to change too. I'm just saying if we empower women, we create change from the inside out.

Can you imagine women who have the ability to challenge the status quo and turn it on its head? Can you imagine women who are prepared with strategies to deal with gender inequality issues while, or even before, they occur?

Change will occur if women are set up to succeed. That is what this book is all about. What is possible with change? Many things, including personal growth, being able to take a stand for yourself, movement toward your goals, credibility in your field, being listened to, not getting taken for granted, not being overlooked, not treated as second best, and much more.

I want women to never be without the secrets of success in the workplace again. I want women to learn how to effectively challenge the status quo. I want women to transform the way they think, act, and work with others to reach their goals.

3

THE SECRET TO IT ALL

What I'm going to start this book with is critically important. Without understanding this, you are never going to be able to fully use the tools, ideas, and solutions from this book.

You are only as successful as your confidence will allow.

Why do I say this? And why is this the key to it all? If you don't have confidence in yourself—confidence in your talents, confidence in your ability to communicate, and confidence in your ability to follow through—you are not going to be as successful as someone who does.

Men are generally more confident than women, which is the biggest reason why this secret is the key to it all.

If your confidence falls below your male counterpart's, you will never be considered equal.

This is a huge revelation to most women. And it is the truest statement you will probably ever read on the topic of gender equality.

Unless you have been hiding under a rock, you have heard and read about how girls are treated and are raised differently than boys from the time they're born. Simply put, girls in our culture are traditionally not raised to be strong, dominant, and confident women. This, of course, is an over-generalization as I know many parents, teachers, and coaches who are doing it differently because they recognize the need to.

We can blame society and our culture for how we were raised. We can focus on the negative and dwell on why this is the way it is. Yet, I think we are better served to think about and act on how to change this about ourselves.

Only you know where you are on the spectrum of self-confidence. And only you know what triggers dips in your confidence or boosts it. This is an intensely personal barometer for each and every one of you. Some women aren't even aware their self-confidence is lacking. Some are aware and overcompensate for their lack of it. Yet we all know people who we admire for their confidence and wish we could be more like.

Being able to evaluate your self-confidence is a great skill and can bring positive results in your life. I was never really good at sports and I knew that about myself, so naturally as a schoolgirl I was never very confident about my abilities in gym class. It never felt good being the next to last person picked for teams. But there is a difference when it comes to self-confidence. It wasn't until high school when I realized that I didn't have to be good at everything all the time to be proud of who I was. Just because I wasn't great in sports didn't mean I wasn't a great person. Knowing and accepting I wasn't great in sports was just a realization of who I was as a person.

It was the beginning of accepting my whole self. In a way, isn't that actually liberating? As it turned out, I didn't enjoy playing sports, but I did enjoy other physical activities such as running, weight training, hiking, yoga, etc. This gave me permission to enjoy what I did like to do instead of beating myself up over not making the team.

Knowing yourself and knowing what areas of your life you aren't great at can also provide you with the opportunity to improve. In the workplace and in life, we aren't going to be able to just "not do" what we aren't the best at. There are skills and abilities you are going to have to be successful at in order to function at work. If you know you fall short in an area, you are going to have to do what is needed to improve. This might be in supervision, organization, managing priorities, communication, public speaking, etc. You aren't going to be able to avoid improving yourself in the workplace like a high school girl can avoid going out for the basketball team. This is the real world after all; put your big girl panties on and get to it.

Confidence comes in many forms and your confidence will vary depending on the situation or area. You can have confidence in one area of your life and lack it in another. Maybe you have tremendous confidence in being able to throw together a great casserole your whole family will enjoy but can't get a cake to turn out even if your life depended on it (this is totally me, by the way). Maybe you have tremendous confidence in managing the budget at work, but fall apart if you have a performance issue you have to handle with one of your employees.

Confidence is truly a personal matter and only you know where you stand.

Many people have a public persona with its own level of confidence and how they choose for other people to see them. Our personal persona can be in stark contrast to our public persona or it can have similarities. People who are experts in how to build confidence highly suggest creating these two personas.

My public persona always has more confidence than my personal does. I will share with you, it is always easier for me to be confident at work than to be confident in my parenting abilities or in being a great wife. The difference for me is the relationships in my personal life mean more to me than those in my professional life. And my roles in my personal life always felt more important to succeed at as well. But when I was down with low self-esteem and confidence in my personal persona, it always bled into my public or work persona. My point is, it doesn't matter how hard you try—both personas play into each other and can be next to impossible to truly keep separate.

When it comes to dealing with the types of issues in the workplace that I described in the quiz in Chapter 1, the confidence you will need to succeed is the kind that is holistic to your entire being. It's the type of confidence made from the sum of the parts. It's the overall attitude, the aura, the spirit, you possess and emanate to the world around you.

If the sum of the parts of your overall confidence is very low, you need to pay attention and work to change this about yourself. If the sum of the parts of your whole is mediocre on the confidence scale, then you too need to pay attention and work toward positive change. I'm not going to include a scale for you to determine where you fit. If you are truly honest with yourself, you will know where you are and you will know what you need to work on.

Self-actualization to improve your overall confidence is hard work and it will take time. You need to be patient with yourself and give yourself permission to develop this over time. But don't take too long or you will miss out.

Please know I don't mean for you to have the same exact confidence level as the men you work with. We all know people whose confidence is to the level of arrogance and this is not what I wish for you. Your level of confidence needs to be equal to the task, the problem, the issue, or the expertise needed at hand to give you the ability to know you can deal with it, do it, lead it, and perform it.

Many people go with the quick fix of "fake it until you make it."

This might be great advice for some things in life. In the matter of self-confidence needed in the workplace to deal with gender inequality, this isn't the place for it. People will see through it if it isn't real and genuine. Most people who "fake it to make it" can't be consistent with it, which causes huge problems. And furthermore, it won't hold up under intense situations, stress, and pressure. And lastly, once someone exposes your confidence as fake, you will face lasting consequences.

Work with the confidence you do have at this point in your life. Always work toward increasing your level of confidence, which should be a life long effort. As you build more confidence, continually bring it into your fold to use toward your success.

No one can build your confidence for you. There may be many people like your significant other, your parents, or your best friend who all may be very good at giving compliments or what feels like are words to help boost your self-esteem. In all reality, this only helps in the short term as your brain doesn't accept it as reality in the long-term. This is especially true if you don't believe it yourself.

As with understanding your confidence level, growing your confidence is also going to be different for everyone. There are lots of self-help books, websites, blogs, and experts to use to help you. Do an Internet search on "how to increase your self-confidence" and you will find many resources. If you are truly serious about increasing your confidence, you will seek out the help you need to do so. If you aren't serious, you won't. This work is up to you. My advice is to get real with yourself and do the work. You'll be glad you did, especially in the long run.

As it relates to women facing challenges in the workplace, I think the following types of actions are most beneficial at increasing your confidence with lasting results and results that will help you be more successful in the workplace. There are more resources on how to build confidence and a thirty-day confidence building program available on my website you are encouraged to check out:

www.WomanToWomanSolutions.com/30-day

Remove the negative self-talk and doubt – Focus on the positive aspects about yourself. Focus on the positive changes you are making. Forgive yourself and replace it with how you will improve yourself for the next time. Never give up or accept mediocrity. And create positive affirmations to repeat and remind yourself you are destined for more.

Get to know and like yourself – Learn who you really are. Accept yourself for the great person you are and the even greater person you want to be. Listen to your thoughts or journal for a better understanding of what makes you tick. Make an action plan to work on your limitations. And lastly, enjoy the process of becoming a better you.

Be prepared – Learn all you can about your field, especially for the job you are in and the job you hope to land in the future. You need to be ready to perform the job to the best of your abilities and to do so, you need to increase your overall knowledge and competence.

There are many ways you can do this. I've used all of them— sometimes all at once. I have found myself taking work home to read manuals and handbooks, the latest research and literature, and policy and procedure papers. I took work home (and did not charge my time) most often for new jobs and promotions where I had so much to learn and I wanted to "hit the ground running." I realize this isn't always possible as there are so many other obligations and priorities limiting your ability to do so. Many of you may even have a second job you have to rush to.

There are other ways to be prepared while you are on the clock at work. Most of us have colleagues we can ask questions or get feedback from. There are usually many employees who have a tremendous knowledge base to tap into, so don't be afraid to do so. People love being asked about their experience, their skills, and their abilities. People also love being asked for their advice. It is human nature to want to talk about ourselves or what we know, so use this to your advantage.

You can also volunteer yourself at work for special projects or assignments that stretch your experience and/or comfort zone. You can use this as a way to work on an area where you may be weak.

Presentation – Use body language to your advantage. Stand up straight; pull your shoulders back. Make eye contact with people when you meet them or are conversing with them (even in a group setting). Use your words to convey confidence by slowing down your speech pattern, and use a tone and volume so you can be heard easily.

* * * * *

I can honestly say that confidence was never my strong suit. It has been a life long process for me to continually keep what confidence I do have and gain more so I can perform at the level I need to and succeed in all the roles I serve. I grew up in a home that was judgmental and critical, so it felt like no matter what I did, it wasn't good enough.

In eighth grade I decided to do a research paper on child abuse, which at that time in the mid-1980s was an emerging social issue being brought to light. As I was telling my mother about what I had learned, my mother slowly explained to me that she was an emotional abuser and how sorry she was she had been hurting me my whole life up till then.

She explained that she was breaking the cycle of abuse and to her credit, she worked very hard to do so. I will always respect her for being honest and being determined to break the cycle as I'm sure it wasn't easy. Yet being emotionally abused at home greatly affected my confidence and my feelings of worth and value as a child. Yet as an adult, I made a choice to not allow this to affect my life, particularly not my confidence or my sense of worth. In addition, I also made a choice to not blame my parents. Blaming doesn't give you confidence. I never used how I was raised as an excuse. It did explain a lot about why I was so challenged with my confidence growing up and the work I had to do to remove the negatives from my thinking.

I fought the insecurities of a young female who did not look the part of a forester working in a male-dominated field. I fought the urge to fall apart and shrivel up inside every time someone critiqued my work or looked at me wrong. I would routinely go blank when put on the spot and had to learn ways to overcome this. I didn't initially know how to stand up for myself or use my voice to say what I meant or what I knew. Yet I wanted a career in natural resources and to excel in my field and in leadership. I didn't have all the tools at first, I just knew what I wanted.

Throughout high school and college I was a "B" student at best, and I had to work hard for those grades. As a result, I never considered myself to be smart. I knew I had to work for everything. Science was my worst subject in school, yet I joined a field requiring a scientific mind and analytical problem-solving skills. I feel like I had to rewire my brain to create the aptitude I needed to build the educational foundation and scientific mind for my chosen career. This was hard work and forced me to overcome a lot of setbacks along the way.

Despite struggling with confidence, I did put myself "out there" and had lead roles in the high school play, sang a solo for a talent contest, became class president, and served as an officer on our student council. I took on leadership roles which I felt very comfortable doing. I truly believe it was these leadership roles that shaped my future for the types of choices I made in adulthood. Thank goodness for these opportunities and parents and teachers that supported me.

I took a summer job at the age of sixteen on a trail crew maintaining backcountry hiking and pack trails accessing public land. This job helped me to build a tremendous amount of confidence as I learned how physically strong and mentally tough I was (try spending a week working and camping in tents in the woods in the pouring rain never being able to get dry or stay warm). This too was a turning point in my life as I could see myself working in natural resource management in a professional role. Once in college, I became the trail crew foreman (or forewoman!) and fought fires on an engine crew.

While in college, I met the man I would fall in love with and marry. He was the smart ass that sat in the back of the class and thought it was his job to see if he could stump our professors with tough questions. He was also the guy you would find in the lobby of our dorm playing cards the night before a big exam. He was the smartest and most confident person I'd ever met. I was in awe of him and studied him intensely. He was also a turning point in my life as I learned from him; through the behavior and attitude he modeled, I learned what it meant to live with unabashed confidence. Even though I learned a lot from him, there was always something in my life I felt was holding me back—having acne, being overweight, not pretty enough, not smart enough, not capable enough.

I was overweight up until my mid-thirties, which wreaked havoc on my confidence. I was always ashamed of my body and I always felt like my weight was holding me back from what I knew my full potential could be. And I was right, it did affect how I lived my life. As anyone who has lost the weight will tell you, it didn't magically create confidence. It helped, but I still had to work internally to overcome my lack of self-confidence.

There was always a little flicker of fight inside me, and maybe it's in you, too. I don't remember the day or the exact moment, but I remember my life changed when I decided this flicker was going to be a good, roaring campfire. I decided it was time to live my life in a manner that I respected. My life was going to meet my intentions despite what anyone else thought or what circumstances came my way. I made a choice. I chose to not let confidence be a limiting factor in my life. You can too.

Having confidence is a choice. Your past doesn't define it for you. Your perceived limitations don't define it for you either. And your failures don't determine it for you. You determine what your confidence will be for yourself. You define it.

Your confidence and the degree to what you have is on you to create and choose for yourself.

Confidence is the key to it all and now that you know this, the secret to your success, do the work and quit letting it be a limiting factor in your life from this day forward.

4

PURPOSEFUL CONSCIOUSNESS

Purposeful consciousness is my own term and I define it as a deliberate act of checking in internally to find out what is really going on. Or you can think of this as the opposite of being on autopilot. Some people also refer to this as being "present in the moment."

My intent isn't to go all meta-physical on you with this concept, but it's to drive home this important strategy you can learn now to help you in so many aspects of your life.

I recognize it is nearly impossible to go through a day and never be on autopilot. Being on autopilot isn't a negative as it has its place in our reality. However, the challenge is knowing when to break from autopilot to being present in the moment. This is the reason why I use the word "purposeful" as I describe this concept.

Given our extremely busy lives, demands placed on us, and all the hats we wear, we purposely need to remind ourselves to downshift to the present moment.

What does being purposefully conscious do for you? It can help you make better decisions and allow you to react to your circumstances in a manner you consciously choose (as opposed to having to put your foot in your mouth). It can make you aware of what might be really going on emotionally that's causing you to feel a certain way. Understanding what is really going on inside you gives you the chance to ensure you present yourself physically or verbally to others in a manner of your choosing. Being purposefully conscious also gives you a chance to recognize when you need to slow down and watch other people's behavior and reactions to determine how to best engage them.

Before realizing how great being purposefully conscious is in life, I relied on self-control or willpower. Self-control and willpower are different from purposeful consciousness as purposeful consciousness is actually taking both self-control and willpower to a higher level.

Here is an example. If you are only using self-control when dealing with a frustrating co-worker, you might find yourself saying, "Today I am not going to let him push me to the point of anger." What happens when you lose your self-control? When you use purposeful consciousness, you are actually monitoring your emotions and become aware of your frustration before it gets to anger. This allows you to make a choice in how you wish to handle the situation rather than responding with a knee-jerk reaction.

Here is another example I'm sure many of you can relate to. How many of you have relied on willpower only to find yourself having eaten a full-size bag of chips without even realizing it? Willpower really came through for you there didn't it? Yet, when you are present in the moment you are at a place where you aware enough to know you really don't want to sabotage your diet with a whole bag of chips and can ask yourself what the real reason is for the emotional eating. When you are honest about what is really going on, it allows you to work through your emotions and feelings toward a positive result or to make another choice.

Being purposefully conscious gives you a chance to evaluate the situation, figure out what is really going on, and to choose how you wish to respond.

Purposeful consciousness is an action you invoke, and until you exercise it often, it is hard to remember to use. My recommendation is start learning how to be purposefully conscious as you go about your daily life. Begin with simple routines in your life. For example, start in the morning as you brush your teeth and be fully engaged in the experience for a few seconds. It sounds stupid, but it's a great way to begin forming a new habit or practice for yourself. My favorite time to use my purposeful consciousness is when I take the first sip of coffee in the morning. I love that feeling of warmth, the newness of the day, and the smell. As you use your purposeful consciousness more throughout your day, it will be easier to remember and easier to use. It will become a natural part of who you are.

* * * * *

Along with your purposeful consciousness, there is another concept that goes hand in hand.

When you are present in the moment you have the opportunity to choose your own response. The situation doesn't choose your response, you do.

A challenging person in your life doesn't choose your response, you do. You are in control of your responses.

If you are like me, you like to be in control of as much of your world as you can. Being in control makes me feel better. Notice I don't use the word "power." I see control and power as two very different things, yet I know how interconnected the two words are as well. I like the kind of control where I have the ability to make my own decisions and transform something into what I want it to be. I like having control over what I eat, when I exercise, what I spend my money on, where I live, what I learn, who my friends are, how I vote, etc.

What do we have control over really? Many of you have influence over aspects of your job, even if you are not a manager or supervisor. Even if your job is solely to take people's order and money at the local burger joint, you have control over how clean your counter is, how you treat customers, how well you listen to get their order right, etc. Perhaps you have influence over what they order if they ask questions. You might even have influence in making improvements or efficiencies in your job if your supervisor is open to it.

Most of us have influence in our home, whether it's over a major decision like picking out the home that is right for us or a minor one like keeping it clean, choosing the paint color on the walls, etc. How about our kids? We really don't have total control over our kids, but we do have control over our parenting. As parents, we have influential power in how we raise them. And we sure enough have control over the keys to the car when they're teenagers.

The biggest reason I like knowing what I can control in my work setting is that I can think through what options I have going forward. I use it as a proactive approach to solving issues or things I don't like. If I don't like how my boss just treated me, I have an array of choices I can make. I can choose to discuss the matter right away, choose to document the incident and hold off, evaluate if this is just a one-time occurrence or a pattern I need to be aware of, determine if I pushed a button and triggered something I will make sure I never do again, etc.

Knowing what I can control allows me to be proactive rather than being reactive. It allows me to choose my responses to circumstances, people, or the crisis of the minute. This is of great value because it gives me a sense of peace, a say in the matter, and a good feeling about moving in the right direction. This shift in focus moves me from what I can do rather than what I don't have control over. This shift is positive and also affirms that I am putting my energies and concentration on the right thing. Knowing what you can control can do the same for you.

* * * * *

I'm introducing some new concepts, habits, and ways of thinking to become part of your life and become part of who you are as a person. It's easy to gloss over these first few chapters and say to yourself, "I'll do that later" or "This isn't important right now" or "I don't want to." Let me assure you, if you choose to ignore these first few chapters you aren't going to achieve the results and success this book talks about. You will be cheating yourself. You will be cheating yourself out of greatness. Embrace the changes you need to make and do them for yourself. You are worth the effort you put into yourself. I believe that and you need to as well.

Look at yourself in the mirror and get honest and real. Use your purposeful consciousness and your influence of what you can control to create the confidence you need inside you so you can effectively and successfully be the woman you want to be at work and in life.

5

YES, IT'S A MAN'S WORLD

Working for twenty-five years in natural resource management, there is no doubt it is a male-dominated field. Generally in this field, one-third of employees are female and there are even fewer females in middle and upper management positions. It is a field where we regularly work with things such as chainsaws, hand tools, fire engines, and helicopters. Typical daily attire in the workplace is leather boots and hard hats. How much more of a "man's world" can you get?

Honestly, I've gotten extremely comfortable working in a setting where I was the only female at a meeting or on a crew. Slowly during my career, I began to notice more females joining me in the ranks, but for the longest time, I was it.

I knew full well the field I chose to work in was male dominated and yet it didn't deter me at all. By nature, I was never afraid when the odds were stacked against me. I was never afraid to work in a career typically held for men. Growing up, my father always told me I should marry a veterinarian or a forest ranger because of my love for animals and the outdoors. He meant well; his generation didn't think about women in the workplace as we do now. Telling his only daughter who to marry was not discriminatory or limiting in his mind, it was the only reality he knew. Inside, however, I would tell myself I would just become one. I knew, even at a young age, I could become whatever I wished and didn't need a man to marry into it. I knew I wanted to be a little unconventional and it sparked a fire in me.

The summer before my junior year of high school I landed my first job in natural resource management. I was very excited and eager to learn. That summer would be the first time young high school girls were hired for a trail crew at that office. Our job was to clear and improve trails in the forest using hand tools. We hiked and camped overnight for four to five days at a time using llamas as our pack animals. It was a great experience as I got to see some of the most beautiful country I'd ever seen. I also learned a lot about myself, how strong I was and how much endurance I had.

Three weeks into the job I learned the men in the office had placed a bet on how long I and the other female high school student on the crew would last. They doubted our ability to handle camping, the extreme conditions we would be exposed to, and the hard work. I admit it was tough, yet I never for a second thought about quitting. Apparently, many of the men had bet that we wouldn't make it past two weeks. So when we showed up for work on the third week, there was a lot of commotion when money was lost. I don't know the exact details of how much money was bet against us, who lost money, or who bet for or against us. It honestly didn't matter or bother me either. I was too proud of the work we had accomplished and who I had become because of it. My attitude towards it was "serves them right to lose money" and "I'll show them." I think I carried myself a little taller and a little prouder from that day forward. I had literally beaten them at their own game.

I continued to work in natural resource management each summer through high school and college. I approached each job in the same manner too—proud to be a woman and proud to be in a field that worked hard and made a difference. I most definitely had a lot of confidence in myself, and I'm sure it showed to everyone.

What I realized early on was the advantages of being a woman (or a being a girl in my younger years) in a man's world.

Yes, it's true; there are advantages to being a female working in a man's world.

The first advantage I learned with the men betting against me was that we often hold the element of surprise on our side. We have all heard stories about women who succeeded despite the odds or succeed when a man couldn't and you've been utterly and completely impressed by them. I see women firefighters do this all the time as they work as hard as their male counterparts. It never fails; the men always say something about how impressive they are for their strength, endurance, and skills. Deep down and while they may not admit it, I think men look at a woman doing a physical job and doubt her abilities to perform at a high level. They don't expect it and when we exceed expectations, they sometimes can't help but say something out loud.

So, ladies, we have the element of surprise when we perform at a high level. This can be a good thing as it gets us noticed so much faster than our male counterparts. Standing out can be a very good thing if it means more opportunities. Many men can spend months and even years trying to stand out above the competition, just waiting for the right opportunity to shine above the others. Fortunately (and unfortunately), sometimes women just have to perform to the same level as an average man to stand out.

The second advantage I see in being a woman in a man's world is our ability to communicate. Both men and women have the capability of being good communicators. However, women tend to have the advantage and are generally better at communicating. We still need to be aware of how we communicate, particularly in making sure we are articulate. But women can use this advantage to ask good questions, be good listeners, be excellent presenters, be great leaders, and be able to speak on many different levels and subjects related to your business.

Women, in general, don't let egos get in their way. Women don't tend to be driven by their ego or have their ego to blame for their demise. As such, I think women tend to be more open to the potential in people or opportunity in situations. When someone isn't distracted by their ego, they can be much more strategic, focused, and driven.

Women are naturally more inclusive and are hardwired to create relationships with others. The relationships we build generally go beyond the boardroom and are multi-dimensional. Our relationships are often long lasting and supportive, which means it's important to us to see both sides benefit. As such we are specialists in networking, which is the natural place we turn to for testing ideas or problem solving.

Because women naturally build a larger and more diverse network, we tend to have better career capital too. Being more inclusive means we will have more varying perspectives to work with which is highly advantageous in today's global market and interconnected business environment.

Yes, we women are more emotional than men, yet this enables us to be much better at picking up cues such as body language and the emotional meaning behind it. Women are like a beacon to emotional stress, pain, tiredness, and much more. And women are often more compassionate about others' feelings, which tends to build stronger relationships and healthier working environments.

All of these advantages are attributes of an effective leader and allow women to achieve success on a different plane than most men. Women leaders tend to be big-picture thinkers and are able think and act multi-dimensionally. This is different than our male counterparts as they tend to think and act in a more linear fashion and are often more narrowly focused. This also means our leadership style can also be more innovative and creative.

Let's face it, we have advantages I like to call "gifts." Man's world or not, our gifts can (and should) be used to benefit us. These gifts were given to us for a reason, so let's use them.

6

HOW TO BE TAKEN SERIOUSLY, DESPITE BEING A FEMALE IN A MAN'S WORLD

Not being taken seriously is such a common issue for all women no matter what seniority level they are, how many years of experience they may have, or how many credentials they may have earned. If you are female in the workforce long enough, you will likely run across the issue of not being taken seriously at least once in your career and probably many times.

In my opinion, the following are some of the most common areas in which women can make huge improvements in how they are perceived so that they're taken more seriously.

Know your stuff – A surefire way to be taken seriously is to make sure you know your stuff. I don't mean fake it. I mean truly know your job inside and out and be an expert at what you do. It doesn't matter if your job is flipping burgers or managing financial accounts.

You need to know how to do your job extremely well. Why is this so important? Simply put, mediocrity doesn't cut it. Mediocre can be replaced by someone else. The biggest reason you need to know your stuff is because you won't be respected in your profession or field if you don't perform your job to the best of your ability. Being respected is a direct link to being taken seriously.

For some professions, you may be required to use your physical abilities. This may mean you need to step up your fitness level in order to perform better. The jobs requiring both physical and cognitive function can be double the amount of preparation it takes to being great at your job. If this is the case, make sure you don't leave one behind and expect the other to compensate for it. This is simply not going to work, especially in a man's world. In a man's world the physical aspects of the job are likely a lot easier for most men, so yes, they do have a leg up on women. Yet when women can meet and exceed the physical demands and skills for a job *and* perform excellently using their cognitive abilities, we indeed can make quite an impression. Often, a lasting impression.

As a new district manager, I met up with the five-person trail crew who worked for me one afternoon. None of them knew I used to work on a trail crew in my younger years. I would say the crew had respect for me as a person in the position as district manager, but let's just say the respect went through the roof when I put my work gloves on and began working side-by-side with them cutting logs out of the trail with a crosscut saw and using an ax to chop downed trees in half. This is a great example of where being excellent at my job using both my physical and cognitive abilities paid dividends in the respect department.

Be confident in yourself – This tip has certainly been discussed at length in a previous chapter, but I need to drive it home again. If you know your stuff and are excellent at your job, then you have every reason to be confident. So have confidence in yourself. Make sure you carry yourself in a manner that shows confidence such as having good posture. Use a clear strong voice when you speak to others. Make eye contact and don't be afraid to hold that contact.

Watch your communication style – Pay attention to how (and what) you communicate. If you talk in circles you need to quit doing so as this does not build confidence in those who are listening. Use plain speech to get your point across. Women tend to over-explain how they feel or believe they have to justify their thoughts before they say them. Neither of these are necessary and often detract from or possibly devalue the point you are trying to convey.

I worked with a woman who used baby talk at work. She would say things like, "I have a widdle question." Please tell me how this would ever build confidence or gain other's respect?

Many women do what is called "upspeak" and don't even know they are doing it. They end their statements with a higher tone of voice, making their statement sound like a question. This is a terrible habit as it makes it sound like you need everyone's approval and lack confidence in what you just said.

More and more common are people using text speak or emojis in their communication. Please don't talk to others and end your sentence by saying "LOL." It's OK to just laugh.

I've seen a lot of people try to use big words and complex phrases. These people are trying to sound intelligent. They think if they come off sounding smart and educated, then everyone will think they are and what they have to offer is also. But most often, this backfires. Your best bet is to sound relatable to the average person using straight and simple words in your dialogue. No one likes a smarty-pants or a show-off, and certainly most people aren't too thrilled to have someone talking over their head. I worked with a biologist who talked in scientific terms all the time. I understood him, but what I was nervous about was if the public we served would be able to. Sure enough, I was right. People didn't understand him and got frustrated feeling like they were getting a line of you-know-what or worse, being lied to. So trust me when I say that how you talk at work is how your boss thinks you talk to your customers or clients. Your boss wants simple and relatable communication to ensure trust is built and relationships are improved.

On the flip side, don't start communicating by saying, "This might be wrong, but ..." or "This might not work, but...." It's never good to begin talking about your idea in a negative way. By doing so, you have already tainted the whole idea. Everyone is going to stop listening from the moment you have discounted yourself. If you aren't sure about what you are going to say, then wait until you are sure. If you are afraid of getting rejected, then get some courage and try it anyway. If you find yourself starting out your dialogue in this negative tone, take a look inside yourself to determine what is going on. Recognize that your true issue might be a fear of rejection or a fear of what others might think. Understanding what is really going on can help you understand and deal with the underlying issue. This, in turn, can help you move past your underlying issue so you can move ahead in a more positive and confident tone.

Raise your hand – It's not a bad idea to raise your hand and offer to work on a special project. This can do several things for you. This can show others you are a team player and are willing to lend a hand in service to your organization. People notice this type of volunteering and it gains respect, especially if you are taking on a larger workload because of it. It is also a great way to broaden your horizons, get yourself noticed, and/or help you in an area in which you may be weak.

Be prepared; plan ahead – You can gain a lot of respect from those in your workplace if you are the kind of employee who is always prepared for meetings, thinks through issues before they arise, or has thought through the next phase. Don't underestimate the value of this, and train yourself to think beyond the moment or the current crisis.

Follow through, be accountable, and do what you said you would do – This is one of my pet peeves in the workplace. If you said you were going to have a report done by a certain date, then be accountable and have it done. If you said you would e-mail a document to someone, then do it. Hold yourself accountable for the assignments, deadlines, and commitments made for you by management or your supervisor as well as for those you made for yourself. Return phone calls and be on time too, both of which seem to be a lost art these days.

Don't make excuses for yourself – So when you weren't fully prepared, missed a deadline, or failed to return a phone call, don't blame someone else or make excuses. Everyone, yes everyone, sees through it. Own your mistake, mis-step, or misunderstanding. I, for one, appreciate honesty and a quick and sincere apology. Owning your mistake and apologizing means so much more to people as they consider your relationship than an excuse ever will. It also gives others confidence that your mistake will not be repeated again. Bigger yet, it goes a long way in gaining people's respect when they know you are being honest and not feeding them a line.

When at work, be fully at work – This is getting harder and harder for employees, especially when your smartphone is constantly notifying you whenever someone "liked" your photo on Facebook, when there is a new update for your favorite app, another personal e-mail comes in, etc. If you have to put your phone away to keep from getting distracted then do so. I guarantee that if you spend any amount of time at all on your device, people are noticing. And, if you are on your device, people will always assume it is personal, even if it's not. As a result, you may be getting a reputation for being on your personal device all the time, which is not positive. I highly recommend you turn off all your notifications and sounds while you are a work (turning your phone on vibrate isn't the same thing as turning it off).

Your professional image says a lot – Many employers are becoming more casual in their dress code, which many employees greatly appreciate. Most people have a style they naturally gravitate to and I recommend you evaluate your own sense of style. The way you dress at work can say a lot about your confidence (or your overcompensation for it). How you dress tells people how you want to be perceived, your commitment, and it ultimately contributes to whether or not you are taken seriously at work.

I have worked with several young firefighters who would show up at my office ready to go to work on a fire. However, they didn't look like it because they were wearing flip-flops or sandals. They had all their other fire protective clothing on, but did not have the right footwear on. When I would ask them about it, they would tell me their socks and boots were in the truck. In their mind, they were ready. Their image said the opposite to me. In my mind, I immediately saw them as unprofessional. I even discounted their knowledge and ability to lead people and perform their job. And I sure didn't appreciate having to pay them to finish getting dressed before they got on the truck. Needless to say, it didn't take long before the word got out about what I thought of this. Not only did these two gentlemen change their ways, but I rarely had another firefighter show up for a fire assignment with flip flops or sandals on again.

My professional image has changed over time. When I first started working I wore what most foresters do when they spend most of their time in the woods with trees. Even if I was in the office rather than working outside, I generally wore the same attire. Come to think of it, I wore the same thing on the weekends too—hiking boots, jeans, a t-shirt, and a sweatshirt if it was cool. My jewelry was limited to my wedding ring and small earrings that my dad gave me for my sixteenth birthday.

After a few promotions, my job changed to include more program development, budgeting, and planning which meant more time in the office spent supervising and leading teams. As a result, I did make changes to my professional image and was excited about those changes too. I began wearing casual business attire and traded out of the hiking boots into something with a wedge or a heel. I still wear casual business attire today—yes, even on the weekends because it feels like me. And I enjoy jewelry—nothing big or flashy, but I have a nice collection I rotate through rather than just the one pair of earrings.

The one constant over the years is mascara, which I wear day in and day out. Even if I were on a fire assignment I would put my mascara on before hitting the fire line each morning. This probably sounds funny, but mascara was my thing that made me feel like I was ready to present myself to the world and take it on. Still to this day, I wear it seven days a week. My mascara sure doesn't get a day off. Maybe it's too materialistic of me, but I love the way I look when I wear it, and I love the way I feel when I wear it. It is not just part of my professional image, it's part of the image that is me.

You may have worked for someone or with someone who said you need to be more feminine. Or maybe it was the opposite, and you were told you need to be less feminine. I've never quite known what to think as I've been told both of these things. I don't know what to think because I want to say, "Make up your mind will you!" Yet my response is always the same: "Hey, I am who I am." I show up in fire clothes ready to go fight fire and I'm told I should be more feminine. I show up in a dress on a day in the office full of meetings and paperwork and I'm told I should be less feminine. Honestly, these comments just don't matter because they are truly meaningless. Whoever says them is showing their true colors, if you know what I mean. Keep that in perspective when you hear these words said to you. Consider the source, it's likely an idiot. Your professional image can easily accommodate having elements of being more or less feminine depending on your mood, the work at hand, or the conditions. Don't let the source of these comments make you crazy.

* * * * *

If you've done all the things I've mentioned and you still aren't getting the results you want, I'd ask you to take a look inside. Get very honest with yourself and determine if you truly are doing these things and making the necessary changes. One other question to ask is whether or not you respect yourself. If you don't respect yourself, you are going to have a very hard time gaining other's respect as well. As I said before, respect and confidence are intertwined so go back to the chapter on confidence and make sure you aren't living a life short-changed. If you are, it will show up as a challenge as you work on any aspect I mention in the upcoming chapters. Change doesn't occur overnight and you do need to give it some time. Hold your head high as you make these changes, because you are worth the effort and you have such a meaningful future to fulfill.

We can't talk people out of their beliefs.
We can only provide them with a new experience.

This is why I speak to strategies as action, not cheap talk or just words. Your actions to incorporate these strategies, make changes in your life, and improve your situation will create a new experience not just for you but also for everyone around you. In fact, you don't have to prove anything. You just need to invoke these strategies to create a new experience for those around you. There is a difference between a new experience and proving yourself, and I hope it makes this feel easier to take on.

Please recognize, there will be idiots and just plain mean people in your workplaces. These can be men or women. You may find you are working with someone who is to his/her core angry, full of rage, deceitful, and otherwise rotten. These people, no matter what strategy you employ, will always be trouble. Unfortunately, this may mean you will need to get out of the situation as soon as you can. I know this isn't fair, but a toxic individual is unlikely to improve over time. You leaving may be your only option to save your health and your sanity. Only you know how much you can tolerate and how long you can exist in a toxic environment. And you will need to use this to determine when and how to find a graceful exit.

I know this sounds strange, but toxic individuals need our prayers. They are sad and miserable people when you think about it. To live life as they do must be the worst thing ever. Their whole goal in life is to have control over others, create chaos, work to bring out the worst in people, and find the negative in all situations. It just has to be exhausting for them, yet that isn't our problem. It is *their* problem! We spend most of our time giving them our power because we let them make us miserable. So if you are going to stay in a toxic environment even if it's only until you can find a way out, as hard as it is, you need to maintain your composure and your integrity. And most importantly, you need to rise above their crap and not allow it to make you so miserable you lose sleep or your stress levels jump through the roof. Remember, it is your choice to choose the response to any situation. Regardless of how bad it gets, it's your choice how you react and move forward. Don't give away your choice; make it for yourself.

Your voice matters and your contributions matter. You need to be heard when you communicate. In life, not everyone is going to listen to you despite your best efforts to communicate extremely well.

Do everything you can to ensure you are communicating effectively and being taken seriously.

Make sure the world doesn't miss out on what you have to say just because you didn't do your part.

7

TOO AGGRESSIVE OR BOSSY? THANKS FOR THE COMPLIMENT

Our culture has a fear of seeing women succeed in leadership roles. So remember this: being told you are too aggressive or too bossy in a leadership role is likely a response based in fear, not fact.

I have been told countless times I am too aggressive or bossy. Eventually, I decided I was going to take it as a compliment. My way of thinking became, "Great, I must be doing something right." My mother used to tell me all the time as a little girl how terribly bossy I was. Growing up in the 1970s, it wasn't considered appropriate for a girl to boss everyone around all the time. It wasn't acceptable in the culture I grew up in. I learned to suppress my leadership qualities (also known as bossiness), yet those qualities never left me.

My daughter is very independent and was told by one of her teachers that she's bossy. And we notice at home, even as the youngest in our house, she certainly wants to be in charge most of the time. I'll never forget her coming home from first grade and telling me, "Mom, I'm never going to marry the boys in my class because they don't do what I tell them to do." She wasn't complaining about the boys, she was just stating a fact. There was no way I was going to tell her the boys didn't have to do what she said or that husbands and wives are to be an equal partnership. I figured there was time for that conversation later in life. My response was, "That sounds like a good plan."

I knew what was going on; as one of only two girls in her class, she was the leader of her group and I'm sure she did most of the organizing of play on the playground and such. There is just no way I was going to squelch the leadership qualities she was developing. That would be wrong, just as it is wrong that many girls across this country have leadership qualities being driven out of them too. I want my daughter and all girls to be comfortable and confident in their leadership qualities, not be batted down as soon as they make a positive move.

* * * * *

My advice to you if you are told or accused of being bossy or too aggressive is to stay the course. You are doing something right. You are bucking the system and the culture in which we work. It isn't easy, but you are doing it. Stay bold and stay the course.

* * * * *

A few months after taking a new position, my supervisor took me to lunch. I thought this was awfully nice, but I realized immediately after ordering that he took me to a public place so I wouldn't react. He proceeded to tell me I was too aggressive and that it bothered people in his office (never mind the fact that I didn't even work in his office; I worked sixty miles away). He also had a detailed plan for me detailing how he would like me to back off and try a gentler approach. The whole thing was despicable, to say the least.

I listened to him, as he was my supervisor after all. I thanked him for his input and told him I would carefully think about his constructive criticism. And I did think about it for the entire sixty-mile trip back to my office. I documented the conversation so I would have it to refer to if I ever needed to, as some of his statements I considered crossed the line from gender inequality to discrimination. I went home and told my husband about it which validated my next response, which was to stay the course.

A few months later we had the worst fire season my district had ever had and my leadership role was certainly challenged, yet I was on top of my game. Funny how my supervisor never mentioned I was too aggressive then; in fact, he was complimentary.

* * * * *

Here is another thing to remember when you get comments or criticisms like this: it is highly likely the individual or individuals you are receiving this from are doing this to purposely throw you off your game. Be very careful when you decide how you are going to respond. Think about it; why else would someone make a comment or criticism such as this if they weren't purposefully testing you to see what your reaction will be? Wouldn't they love it if they could bring insecurity into your mind and rock your world? Wouldn't they love it if your performance dipped? Wouldn't they love it if you over-reacted and made a fool of yourself? This is why it is so critical to stay the course. Don't feed them what they want. Don't let them see how their criticism has rocked your world. Don't go around second guessing yourself. Don't run around asking everyone you work with to validate what was said about you. It will be tempting and is likely human nature to do these things, yet remember you are the one in control of how you react and choose to respond. This means you have it within you to stay the course.

Staying the course has always worked for me. And it will likely work for you too. However, it is never a bad idea for some self-reflection and earnest evaluation when someone gives you this feedback. Are you being too aggressive for the situation? Could you be overly aggressive or bossy as a means to over-compensate for other areas or shortcomings? Is your personality too strong and might need a slight tuning down?

Only you are going to know the true answers to these questions, so I do challenge you to be honest with yourself with any feedback you receive including the "too aggressive or bossy" feedback.

If you have received this feedback because you believe you are doing something right, thank the individual for giving it to you and tell them you will consider it carefully. Then be on your merry way, staying the course.

8

NOT GETTING THE SAME OPPORTUNITIES AS YOUR MALE COUNTERPARTS? CREATE YOUR OWN!

If your work environment is anything like many companies and organizations in today's working world, you see men getting more opportunities than women. It isn't fair. It isn't right. And yes, something should be done about it to change the culture.

Yet here are the surprising facts.

Your future is in your hands, ladies.

If you feel you are being held back or not getting the same opportunities as your male counterparts, then you need to take control and do something about it. My favorite advice to share with people is, "You have to look out for number one because no one is going to do it for you." You can never rely on your supervisor or training manager to do this for you. You cannot wait for others.

You have to make this happen on your own.

Do you have a training plan you have created for yourself and shared with your supervisor? If not, you needed to do that yesterday. You need to chart your course in how you are going to go from point "A" to point "B." This needs to include building your skills, your knowledge base, your experience levels, your qualifications, your certifications, or whatever is needed for your particular job or next job you are trying to land.

Ask people in your organization what they did to get to where they are. Find out the qualifications needed for promotions you are interested in. Determine how to get the knowledge, skills, abilities, experience, training, etc. you need to get you where you are going.

This area is a great place for you to be "too aggressive." There is nothing wrong with being aggressive and it might even be necessary to ensure you get a fair crack at training and opportunities.

After you have created your plan, share it with your supervisor. You and your supervisor need to have a one-on-one conversation about your plan. It needs to be a discussion where you come to a mutual agreement. You need your supervisor's support, so you need to enlist him/her to help you in your quest.

You also need support from your peers as you might be competing with them for the budget to send you to training that is costly. You might be competing with them if there are only so many open slots available in a given year. You need to work together to find some common ground in how you can support each other so you all can move up the ladder.

You also need support from those you may supervise, as they are likely the ones who will be taking on your duties and assignments while you are away in training or on a special assignment. One surefire way of gaining their support is by being the kind of supervisor to them you would want to have. You need to work with them in their employee development and training needs as well, just as I'm instructing you to do for yourself.

Sometimes your supervisor won't want to support your plan or parts of your plan, which means you need to find out why. A colleague of mine decided she wanted training and to begin building her career in a completely different direction than her current job/career was going. She was frustrated with her supervisor for not supporting her and not allowing her to attend expensive training and take assignments so she could become certified. What she wasn't doing was putting herself in her supervisor's shoes. Her supervisor couldn't support her plans because there was no budget for training outside her current position, and if he let her go on assignments he had no one to do her work. So what looked like a lack of support was actually due to things outside the supervisor's control given the budget and workload impacts. As a result, she worked with her supervisor on finding other sources of funding as well as people willing to cover her workload when she left on assignment. The lesson to this story is to ask, rather than assume, what your supervisor is thinking and concerned about. Work with your supervisor to resolve the concerns and you will be much more successful in getting what you want.

As I've said before, there are very bad supervisors out there and if you are in that situation, I am truly sorry. You may be in the situation I wrote about at the end of Chapter 5. If so, go re-read that now.

9

THE OPPRESSIVE ATMOSPHERE MAKES ME FEEL LIKE THERE IS NO RESPECT FOR MY OPINION OR CONTRIBUTION

If you haven't experienced an oppressive work atmosphere, chances are you most likely will. If you've experienced it, you have likely done so many times over. I can't tell you how many times I've sat in meetings and have been talked over, ignored, disrespected, or someone has just repeated (stole) what I said and received credit for it. This is so terribly frustrating, degrading, demoralizing, and confidence shattering.

As hard as it may seem to do, you must realize you can't resolve this situation or prevent it from happening in the future by taking on a "me versus them" attitude. Your default response in these types of challenges might be to fight. However, you might be the type of person who gives up too. Neither is going to get you what you want; in fact, choosing either of these two actions will likely make it worse.

One of our most basic needs in life is to feel appreciated, which includes feeling like you belong and are valued. The emotion you are feeling comes from these three deep-rooted aspects of our human spirit. This is where your purposeful consciousness is needed. You need to check in with yourself about what is really bothering you. What specifically bothered you and why? Recognizing what you are feeling and experiencing is half the battle.

You need to be honest with yourself too. Why were you ignored when you tried to enter a conversation? Why didn't your idea get any traction? Why did you get cut off when you tried to speak? Our society is quick to blame others, but before you go there take a look at yourself first.

My communication in a group setting still, after twenty-five years, feels like it needs more work. I still feel challenged to communicate effectively, and when I am honest with myself I find there are many ways I could have done better.

I have found myself introducing a new idea to a group of leaders where my idea wasn't fully thought through and therefore, I didn't present it with a lot of confidence or conviction. In this case, it's no wonder my idea fell flat. That's is on me, not my gender.

I also have a tendency to provide an opinion, idea, or statement and then explain it and then state it again. It's as if I have to justify my idea and then repeat it several times. Why do I do this? I think it's insecurity in my own value to contribute. This is a terrible way to communicate if you want to be taken seriously and respected, yet I listen to women do this all the time (men too, by the way). When someone communicates this way, we immediately think they are rambling or are mealy-mouthed.

Take your purposeful consciousness to another level and be real with yourself about how you communicate to others, particularly in a group setting. What elements are you lacking that are truly holding you back in how you'd like others to hear you and see you? Don't blame your communication ineffectiveness on being shy or introverted. I have seen many naturally quiet people be very accomplished in their ability to communicate.

It's not easy to look at yourself first, but these types of inquiries are necessary. Are you speaking with confidence? Are you fully prepared with the needed information to fully contribute? Are you rambling and not getting to the point? Are you complaining or being negative when you need to be solution-oriented instead? Are your words emotionally driven rather than fact or reality driven? Is your body language counter to your words? Are you just talking to talk and don't really have anything of value to say? I challenge you to be honest with yourself about why you might have received the response you did.

If you do have improvements to make in your communication, the good news is these improvements are within your control and something you can change. Recognizing it is half the battle. The rest is making the changes needed. You may ask, "How do I speak with more confidence?" Certainly, you need to do the internal work to become more confident inside so it can be portrayed on the outside as discussed in a previous chapter. The other aspect is to be purposefully conscious the next time you engage and want to share your idea confidently. Make a choice to be in the moment and be confident with your tone of voice, sit up straight, and make eye contact.

If you have been honest with yourself and you truly feel you are still being oppressed in the workplace, then it is time to take it up a notch.

In my experience, it is usually only one or two people who treat me as "less than" at the office or in a group setting or meeting. It is rare an entire group will intentionally treat you unfairly, yet I'm not saying this doesn't happen. If you actually break it down, what may feel like "everybody" is actually only "somebody."

A new fire broke out right on the boundary of my district and the neighboring district. As such, my staff and I worked closely with the staff of our neighbors as we developed plans for the days ahead. I had already gone out to the fire and looked it over and knew without any doubt in my mind exactly where it was located. Over ninety percent of the fire was on the district I managed and was responsible for. I had invited the neighboring district manager and his staff to my office to meet and discuss the fire along with our local volunteer and state fire managers and the sheriff's office.

As soon as introductions were over and I initiated the purpose of the meeting, the neighboring fire manager began to disagree with me on the location of the fire. I could tell he did not understand where it was, so I took the time to draw it on a map for him. After drawing it out, he still disagreed with me openly and told me where he thought it was. It was a little troubling being called out in front of all these fire managers and the sheriff's officers (never mind that I was the only female in the room), yet I was confident I knew what I was talking about. It was clear he was not willing to back down; we were at an impasse. We were literally not able to continue the meeting because the differences in opinion about the location of the fire changed the type of strategy we would take.

In this situation, it wasn't "everyone" in the room who wouldn't listen to me and respect that I knew what I was talking about. It was just one person. I could have gotten into an argument with him in front of everyone, but I chose not to. I recognized he had never worked with me before, didn't know my experience/background, and therefore didn't trust me. Would he have trusted me if I had been a male? I don't know, and I'll never know. At that moment in time, if this was truly gender bias, it didn't matter. I needed to resolve the matter quickly.

I asked everyone if we could take a break. It just so happened that one of the firefighters working for me also had worked for him in the past, was someone he trusted. As such, I asked him to join us and show us the current map of the fire. It was located just where I had said it was. This was all it took to get the neighboring fire manager on the same page, and from that moment on he was respectful and cooperative as we continued to work together. The fire manager never said anything about being wrong and never apologized, yet everyone in the meeting knew who was right. I would be wrong if I said there wasn't some sense of satisfaction in being right.

My point in this story is that I was not out to destroy this individual and embarrass him in front of his peers and other incident management partners. If I had done that, he would have never respected or trusted me. I needed to handle the situation to form a positive relationship, thinking about the long-term rather than needing to be proven right in that exact moment. Nothing would have been gained other than short-term gratification if I had called him out publicly. I was assertive and didn't back down, but used another means at my disposal to build a relationship.

* * * * *

It's always a good idea to identify the individual or individual(s) who you think are working against you, disrespecting you, intimidating you, etc., as it is unlikely it's an entire group. As much as we would like to, it isn't in our best interest to point blame or put an individual or individual(s) in their place. What is in our best interest is to determine who we're having an issue with and why. Again, in my story it wasn't in my best interest to say, "Hey, if I were a male, would you still be disagreeing with me about the location of this fire?" His issue with me was he didn't know me or trust me, this was the root of the problem I needed to fix. It was in my best interest to turn him, to gain his trust, and to gain his respect. Sometimes we have to take the high road and act in a manner benefiting the greater good. Getting into an argument with this man or being at odds with this man would not have put the fire out any sooner. In fact, I knew I needed to form a quick and positive relationship for the benefit of all the firefighters working on the ground to ensure their safety, their ability to be effective, and not create any additional stress or tension for them.

Understanding the individual's rationale, motivation, or issue with you is something you need to determine in order to move forward toward a solution that benefits you.

I have had several men in my career who didn't respect me because they felt I was inexperienced or wasn't as knowledgeable as they were. This is incredibly common and could happen regardless of any gender issues on top of it.

I worked with an individual whose trust I thought I'd never gain. I had four strikes against me, and he told me so directly; I was young, I wasn't experienced enough, I wasn't educated enough, and I was a girl. Yes, he actually told me these things. I probably spent the next month avoiding him (OK, hiding from him). When I was working with him, I was so nervous I could barely put two intelligent words together, which certainly didn't help my cause.   Eventually   I pulled myself together, grabbed some confidence, and took him on as a challenge. It didn't happen overnight. In fact, I think it took two years to finally gain his respect. The challenge was with myself and asking myself "Do you think you could win him over?" I knew in my heart if I never did, it didn't mean that I should feel less of myself. It was truly his loss and I knew that. Yet, I had to try as I couldn't have this man continue to berate me whenever he felt like it.

So I spent two years doing simple things like reading new scientific articles on the work we did and then making a point to engage in conversation with him on the article. He never missed an opportunity to talk about new research, new information, etc. Truth be known, he never missed an opportunity to listen to himself pontificate. I knew this about him and used it to my advantage, but in an honest and genuine way because I actually enjoyed our conversations. Since I was the junior forester, I made sure he knew how much I respected his opinion and wanted to learn from him. I would ask questions or bring work to him I wanted to problem solve together. I also got to know him as a person too—learning about his past experience/job history, talking with him about what he liked to do outside of work, learning about his wife and kids, etc. He let me into his personal and professional life. None of what I did was "work." It was about forming a personal relationship with a very well respected "good ole boy." I learned so much from him and have benefited from his advice throughout my career.

You need to determine what motivates an individual to treat you poorly. In this case, it was because I was inexperienced and a girl. I couldn't change my gender, but I sure could keep it from getting in the way and remaining a barrier.

You are going to find all kinds of reasons why some people treat you poorly, and being female may be one of them, but it's not the only one. There is always something else going on. There is always another reason.

One such reason, and a common issue in the workplace, is you may be threatening to them in some way. They feel you are smarter and more driven. They may believe you have the favor of upper management and will get the next promotion. Or it could be something else entirely. It is very tough to know what you should do when it appears your very existence threatens theirs.

It's always hard to know if seeing you as a threat is truly at the heart of their issue, so be careful ever stating this as fact or accusing someone of this. If you suspect this is their issue, there are some things you can do to help. You might be thinking to yourself, "If I were a man I wouldn't have to deal with this." Unfortunately or fortunately, this is a problem regardless of gender. This could occur between two males, two females, a female supervisor over a male subordinate, or a male supervisor over a female subordinate.

The hardest situation is when your supervisor is the one who feels threatened or is the oppressor who makes you feel you have little to no contribution or value. This situation is so much more difficult than if it is with a co-worker or colleague, and you will need to be very careful.

People have a basic need to be appreciated and valued. These are at the heart of most issues people have in the workplace.

If people do not get this basic need met at work, they will react in multiple ways, which may be negatively toward you. Your boss may feel threatened by you and react with problematic behavior. Your boss may not feel appreciated and valued by management, and you end up taking the brunt of his or her frustrations.

For these situations, you need to spend time figuring out what motivates people to come to work each day or what is causing the lack of motivation and problematic behavior. Most often what motivates people is to achieve the feeling of being appreciated. There are other motivations in addition to this such as working toward a promotion or dream job or landing a position on a project they are very passionate about.

* * * * *

I worked with a team leader for a few years who barely tolerated my existence, and whenever he could he would undermine me, call out any flaws or mistakes publicly, leave me out of meetings and critical conversations, tell me one thing and do the opposite, and more. It was miserable. My head was constantly spinning trying to figure out how to work with this individual and succeed in my job. He was intelligent, experienced, organized, and very good at his job, so it made no sense to me why he behaved the way he did with me. In the organization, he was supervised by two people who often had conflicting priorities and goals, which made his job difficult at best. As such, I realized he felt like he wasn't meeting the needs of either supervisor which lead to him feeling under-appreciated. He had been in this job for such a long time, over ten years, which I believe was wearing on him as well. Each time he applied for a promotion, it just didn't come through for one reason or another. This made him also feel like the organization undervalued him and didn't see his potential contributions in a higher leadership position.

After I realized this was going on in his world, I began to think about ways I could help him in both arenas. In meetings with our top management, I would make sure to purposely call attention to his leadership and contributions in a manner that was subtle and effective. Because he was the team leader, it was easy to do this as he was the one who often resolved complex issues we were dealing with. He regularly came up with solutions benefiting all, so I could easily call attention to his contributions and how he was making a difference. My biggest effort toward him was to ensure I always showed him respect, particularly when we were in the presence of management or leadership.

It turns out his career goals were similar to mine, and we both wanted to be promoted to district manager positions. The difference between us was he had at least ten years on me. I was not ready to apply for these positions and he was. I learned quickly that what motivated him to come to work each day was to align himself as best he could for a promotion to a district manager job. After some time, I decided to have a heart to heart conversation with him. I spoke about how I supported his career goals, and how I truly wanted to see him succeed. I explained I was years away from being promoted and was not his competition. We were simply gunning for the same job in the future, but at two different points on the timeline. He responded very well to this conversation and most of his undermining stopped. I say most because he was still difficult and caused me headaches, but it was so much better than before. Our relationship wasn't perfect, but it was respectful and productive from that time on.

You can diffuse most issues when you understand a person's need to be appreciated and valued

as well as learn what motivates their behavior.

Let's face it, as a subordinate, your job is to make your supervisor look good and succeed. You may not like to hear this, because you may feel like it is your job to look good for yourself and succeed. But I guarantee if you don't help your supervisor, they won't help you. This is especially the case if you have a difficult supervisor. I have never succeeded when I have challenged a supervisor. Never. I've learned this the hard way I'm afraid.

This means you have to take the high road, which can be a very hard path to follow. And if you are like me, I have to remind myself of taking that high road over and over so I don't fall into a bad pattern. This is not only difficult, but it can also take a lot of patience and can take time before matters improve. You can do it, but you do have to stay committed.

I had a supervisor who on the first day of the job told anyone who would listen, "I'm only going to be here for eighteen months and then I'll be promoted." As the days and months continued, I learned my supervisor would trample over everyone to get ahead and was rude, played games, and was dishonest. To make matters worse, I also learned my supervisor wasn't competent in natural resource management, which was part of the job's responsibilities. There were so many things I did wrong as I handled this supervisor. My biggest fault was not staying committed. About half of the time I worked hard at making my supervisor look good and succeed. Due to the supervisor's incompetence, this was very hard work and I spent the majority of my time cleaning up messes my supervisor had created. It was hugely challenging trying to stay ahead to avoid mis-steps and more messes to clean up. I found myself letting my supervisor make mistakes, say the wrong things in public, miss a deadline, etc. "Why should I have to overcompensate?" I would tell myself. Yet, it always backfired as it made me look bad too.

Your supervisor's behavior is not an excuse for your poor

performance; you still need to perform to the best of your ability. You have a reputation too, and you don't want your reputation as a high quality employee ruined.

The supervisor I'm speaking about was a female. And when I purposely allowed her to fail, she knew it and it hurt our relationship in a way that still causes my stomach to ache. She lost trust in me, her fellow female in arms. I didn't take the high road and I should have. When she lost trust in me, the first time I made a major mistake she didn't support me. In fact, she threw me under the bus, and because she was higher up in the organization this was problematic for me in more ways than one.

Tail between my legs, I did apologize to her and worked the remainder of our time together trying to regain her trust. My primary goal, and I let her know it, was to help her succeed and move into another position on her eighteen-month timeline. I learned the hard way and changed some behaviors of my own. I refused to complain about her in the workplace because it wasn't becoming to me, and it certainly didn't help the situation. I purposely chose never to go behind her back and spread rumors. I didn't allow myself to harbor resentment or work less. I just couldn't allow myself to be labeled as a whiner or a slacker.

Acknowledge your own negative emotions and manage your own behavior to prevent a result that is self-defeating.

Most supervisors who feel threatened by you or express oppressive behaviors also lack self-confidence. You are not going to change this for them, nor should you try. This is their issue and theirs alone. And it isn't something you should exploit for two reasons. The first reason is because it would be mean and cold-hearted to do so. The second reason is because of the chain of command. You don't really want to expose vulnerabilities of your supervisor as he/she can make your life a living hell. Remember, they are in control after all.

Your supervisor's lack of self-confidence is just something you need to be aware of, not act on.

People are watching how you handle difficult situations and people. By people, I mean your co-workers, the employees you supervise, and those higher up. You have the opportunity to shine like no other in the organization if you can find a way or find it within you to work with a difficult supervisor. I don't mean being a doormat and letting the supervisor walk all over you or treat you poorly. I mean taking your relationship to a good place not seen in the organization before. Believe it or not, you have the opportunity to show influential people in the organization how great you are at handling difficult people and situations and building solid relationships even if they start on rocky footing. This is also an opportunity to show off your collaborative and inclusive nature. "Collaborative" and "inclusive" are the latest buzzwords in business, so to be considered both is really what you want to be in today's workplace. Getting along with your difficult boss might be the very thing that can set you apart from other talented candidates for the next promotion or opportunity.

* * * * *

What do you do when it's not your supervisor making your life difficult, but an employee instead? If you've ever had an employee working for you who doesn't respect you and goes over your head, you know you have a problem. This is a unique problem because the disrespect is below you in your chain of command. This can be challenging and can only be dealt with head on. The nice part is that you are the supervisor so you can give clear direction and put it in writing if needed. The fact is, this is called insubordination. I've only ever had this happen to me once, and it didn't take much for me to correct the behavior. But I did have to do two things. The first was to give clear direction of how I wanted this corrected. And second, I had to talk with my supervisor and ask that he not allow my employees to go over my head. Quite honestly it was harder to get cooperation from my supervisor than it was to correct the behavior of my employee. My supervisor was one who loved to talk with anyone in the organization, regardless of his or her rank and file. And he never heard an idea he didn't like. In the end, this did improve but it took an awareness and persistence on my part to have both parties respect my position and role in the organization.

* * * * *

I've been known to treat difficult co-workers and supervisors as if they were difficult clients. Sometimes this makes it easier for me to take the high road. In a way, it's as if you are the more mature one in the relationship. It has meant I needed to stay one step ahead by anticipating workload and work requests and often thinking/planning several moves ahead to avoid jumbled priorities or deadlines. I've had to identify the triggers or situations that create stress or unwanted behavior and avoid them like the plague. I've needed to support their success and do so publicly. It was on me to learn their communication style, preferences, and pet peeves as well as adjust to them as needed. And lastly, I've needed to determine ways to work around their weaknesses through proactive approaches.

In the end, there are just some supervisors or situations you can't turn and some behaviors you can't ignore. There are times when it is absolutely necessary to have a conversation with your supervisor, and you should do so rather than suffer quietly and be miserable. You want to approach this in an open, non-accusatory manner allowing for open communication. You don't want to march in and place blame.

It's easy to believe supervisors don't want feedback, but many of them appreciate it very much. Most supervisors want you to be happy and thrive at work and are willing to make changes if and where they can. You'd be surprised what a genuine and respectful conversation might do for your relationship as well. You may find you have a new level of trust established and ability to work together. Besides, if you are truly miserable, it doesn't hurt to try. Communication in a professional and respectful manner just may be the ticket to resolving your concerns about a negative and oppressive work atmosphere. Your ability and willingness to communicate may also be the resolution to not feeling respected at work too.

In a future chapter, I talk about bullying and sexual harassment, which is a whole different animal. The advice in this chapter is not meant for those situations.

10

DON'T MAKE ME CHOOSE & THEN PUNISH ME FOR MY CHOICE

So you find yourself in a difficult situation where you are being offered a special assignment out of town and yet your daughter has a dance recital you don't want to miss. What do you do? You tell yourself there will always be more dance recitals to attend or that someone can video it for you which is almost like being there, right? You tell yourself there will be more opportunities at work like this, so you'll just take the next one but in the back of your mind you know this may not be true. So you talk to your boss and thank him for the opportunity, explaining that it isn't the right time. Then you find yourself in the coming weeks being the "mommy priority" and suddenly not being taken seriously and assigned less-than-meaningful tasks.

It's awful, unfortunate, discriminatory, and frustrating to be in this situation. In fact, if feels like someone is ripping your heart in two.

To start with you need to be solid on the type of mother you want to be, which I will talk more about later in this book. But let's be honest with ourselves, if all you are doing is going to work to bring home a paycheck and you don't care about a future or career, then choose family over work every time. That choice is simple. If you do care about your career and future, you have a lot to weigh in your decision. There are no right or wrong answers by the way.

I was on baby number two and was at a turning point in my career where I was on what was called the "manager track." I had gotten "the nod" from upper management and now it was time to take a temporary promotion as a district manager to demonstrate to management that I should be promoted. The timing was interesting as my firstborn was still eighteen months old, and now I was ready to have another baby. I was asked to take an assignment in another state for the next four months to a location that was extremely remote with the nearest medical facility an hour drive away. Given my firstborn had to be delivered by emergency C-section, I was not too excited about the location. I had to turn down the assignment, as there was no way I was going to risk the last trimester of my pregnancy and unborn child. My stomach was in knots as I was on the phone with management explaining my situation, but I also made it clear that after maternity leave I would take the next assignment no matter where it was. I had to make sure they knew I was serious about my next career step.

My circumstances in this case were fairly understandable given how challenged I was in delivering babies. I was fortunate to have an understanding management team giving me a pass on this assignment and five months later giving me another opportunity, which I took. But I haven't always been that fortunate.

I have lost track of how many times I have chosen family over work, but I sure can count the number of times I've chosen work over family. Looking back on my career, I can't think of a time when I regretted choosing family over work. I don't want to be one of those people who wishes I had chosen family more when I look back.

When it comes down to it, our loved ones (friends and family) are the most important aspects of our lives and who are going to be with us through life events and to the end.

I'm not saying you should choose family over work in all cases, because in all likelihood you shouldn't. The reason why after twenty-five years in the workforce I know the number of times I've chosen work over family is because of how much thought I put into the decision, how it made me feel leaving my kids or missing an event, or the preparation I put into it beforehand to make it easier on those I left behind.

My kids have always been pretty accepting of when I've needed to miss an event important to them. In fact, as teenagers now, they have no expectation I will attend every athletic game they participate in. I'm so thankful for their understanding. What I've noticed, especially when they were little, is that when I've known in advance that I'd have to miss their event and prepared them for it, they handled it much better. And certainly it did depend on the importance of the event and how much they were looking forward to it too. If you can have at least one parent attend, this really does make a difference. Another great idea is to record the event to watch later with your kids. And here's another trick, if you have other family that can attend like grandparents, aunts/uncles, etc., see if you can get a good showing for the event which will help ease your not being there.

It's important your children know they are the center of your universe, but it is also important for them to know there are other obligations on your time. It's important they learn to share you as well.

If they are old enough to understand, I think it is also great for them to know how hard you work and the goals you are trying to achieve. Your family wants to help you achieve your goals and you'd be surprised to find how supportive your kids are in the choices you may make in favor of your work.

If you do choose work over family, make sure it is for a good reason and there is a clear gain.

I was asked to attend a national conference and give a presentation, which required a plane flight, a several hour drive from the airport in a car rental, and two overnight stays. I was so honored for the invitation to give a presentation at this national conference that I didn't pay attention to how small venue it was. It wasn't until I arrived the day of my presentation that I realized this "national" conference wasn't a big deal and only had forty participants. I enjoyed the event, but I can honestly say I didn't get much benefit out of attending in either the short or long-term. And what's more, it didn't have any benefits to my career either. I wished I had looked into it more before I blindly accepted. Lesson learned.

On several occasions, I have attended conferences and training out of town for extended overnight stays where, because of my husband's schedule, my mother-in-law came to stay with the kids. I never liked asking for help, yet I never felt bad for leaving the kids with her for one big reason. These opportunities helped my kids have a deep and meaningful relationship with their grandmother which is a wonderful thing. In addition, she loved it and greatly appreciated how we trusted her with our children. It was a benefit to all of us.

Now honestly, leaving my kids with just my husband was always a little nerve racking. What if he forgot something or, heaven forbid, did things differently than I? When the kids were really little, I swear every time I left they would get the stomach flu (by no fault on my husband's part, just bad luck). It got to the point where I would cringe calling home to check on things, crossing my fingers my hubby would tell me "everyone is fine." I can't tell you how bad it feels to hear sick kids on the other end of the phone and a poor husband who is feeling overwhelmed. But it was good for my husband to find out what he could do and for the kids to learn that their dad was great at comforting them too. The biggest benefit was for my husband to know I trusted him.

* * * * *

I know there were plenty of times I was passed over for an assignment because my male supervisor felt I "had a lot on my plate," which was code for "motherhood." There were many times I simply wasn't even given a chance to choose. Sometimes this would really bother me, especially after the second or third time or if it was an opportunity I really wanted. I had to have a discussion with several supervisors who had done this to me, which weren't easy conversations. I first had to make sure I had gotten over my anger and disappointment so I could think more rationally and without blame. Once I was ready I gently explained to my supervisor I noticed I had been passed over, how disappointing it was, and explain the types of opportunities I'd be interested in taking in the future.

Most of the time this simple way of handling the situation did the trick. Once I did have a supervisor try to argue with me about not having the time because of my personal obligations, which I refused to argue with him about. I had to repeat it several times, but I explained I had capacity in both my personal life and professional life to succeed. I explained how he needed to allow me to make the best decision for my family, thus he needed to trust and respect I could do so. I gently explained that he didn't need to make those decisions for me. I also thanked him for his awareness and concern, which was tongue-in-cheek, but it was a means to get him off his defense and focus on how I wanted to be treated.

* * * * *

When I did get opportunities and special assignments, I think it goes without saying that I made damned sure I did an outstanding job and successfully juggled all my other responsibilities at work as well. These opportunities are management's way of testing you, let there be no doubt. So if you get one, you need to over-perform. You need to hit it out of the park. If you know you can't do that, for whatever reason, then don't take the assignment. Doing a mediocre job is worse than turning down the assignment for a good reason.

Bottom line, I want you to look at your choice between work and family in a different light, which will hopefully make these decisions easier for you. Yet you can still find yourself at the bottom of the heap when you've chosen family over work. If this happens, it's important to hold your head up high and not let this affect your confidence or performance. This is easier said than done, but you need to show others and yourself you are strong and can work through difficult situations. Make sure to let your co-workers and your supervisor know why you opted out and express your genuine interest and drive to take the next one.

Be persistent with your goals and maybe, just maybe, be a little aggressive with it too!

11

IT'S EXHAUSTING HAVING TO PROVE MYSELF OVER & OVER AGAIN

Not only do women have to prove themselves over and over again, but we also have to do more to prove ourselves in the first place. There is no question there is a disparity between male and females on this issue. Unlike our male counterparts, if we achieved something it is often because we are seen as lucky not because we've earned it or are qualified for it.

Regardless of how unbelievably frustrating this is, we women need to face the facts. I'm sorry to say, but this is our reality ladies. This is our playing field. It doesn't mean we have to like it, but it is part of the job. I have almost turned it into a game. I actually try to guess which situations I expect this in and if I'm right, I do a little happy "I told you so" dance inside. If I'm wrong, then I'm pleased. I suppose it is bad I judge people before I give them a chance to be decent and fair, but I think it's my way of coping with the twenty-five years of frustration.

My favorite scenario is when I'm being underestimated by someone or a group I'm newly working with. It never fails, particularly if I'm working in a fire management scenario; I'm underestimated in my experience and knowledge. And there is usually some younger male who decides to take it upon himself to "educate" me or goes "back to the basics" to explain. You would think by just my mere presence being in the same room with these people, one would assume I had the experience enough to be there. If I had no experience, I wouldn't be there. But no, it's generally assumed I know nothing and it's almost jaw-droppingly stupid of individuals to go there. And once they do, they certainly lose my respect.

Because this has happened to me so often, I have many different responses I will choose to take depending on the situation. I've been known to just let the young male treat me in that manner until he has made a fool of himself and one of his colleagues who knows me tells him to stop. Often it's the male employees working for me that can't stand to see me treated in this way, and they will stop the behavior from continuing. I've also been known to cut them off and bluntly explain to them I don't need remediation. I do this when time is of the essence or when I just don't have much patience. Sometimes I just cut off the individual, turn my back to them, and continue to speak to others with a confident tone and in technical speak, demonstrating I am competent to be there. And lastly, I've just let it go and allowed for my actions to speak for themselves too.

I've also found if I've proved myself in one area, it isn't enough, and then I have to prove myself in another area too. It's not enough that I proved myself as a competent forester, but then I had to prove I was physically fit to keep up with men hiking mountains all day or that I could hold my own fighting fire. The bar would keep getting raised. I couldn't seem to gain any ground.

If you know you have to prove yourself over and over again, then it does somewhat just become part of your mode of operation. Sadly, this is true. You expect to have to prove yourself when you work with a new team; what you don't expect is to have to prove yourself to your co-workers or boss on the same thing over and over. I had a supervisor continually question my ability to handle difficult situations. It didn't matter if he saw me in action and told me how impressed he was; the next situation to come up he would question my abilities again. Even though I never failed, in all the time I worked for him, he was never convinced.

Expect to have to prove yourself over and over again. You will have to prove it wasn't luck all this time, or that you didn't have help, or somehow you had it easy. I'm sorry this is true, but it is.

Living your life having to prove yourself over and over again for the same things can create a lot of extra stress. It's almost like groundhog day where you are reliving your first day of work over and over. It's a constant burden and stress to work as if you are trying out for the team each and every day.

At some point in your career, you just need to be confident inside with your achievements, your competence, your abilities, and your expertise. If you don't do this, the constant proving yourself will overcome you.

If you are confident inside, it won't matter how many times you have to have a repeat performance because you know you can do so with ease.

I will say, given I've been at this for twenty-five years, it does get better with time. I have definitely noticed the need to prove myself has become less and less over the years. Yet if you are changing jobs and companies, it's possible no amount of experience even at the highest level may help. I think I noticed less and less only because I was with the same organization for so long.

* * * * *

There is a time and place for a little well-placed, modest self-promotion. For the supervisor who could never be convinced I could handle difficult situations well, I'd say, "And because I handled the last situation like this with ease and with a positive end, this one will go the same way."

You do need to be careful using this self-promotion because you can't come off as someone who feels like they always have to explain their resume. This does get old for people and it can be looked at as if you don't have confidence in yourself. You can use simple two-sentence promotions to quickly reference a similar situation related to what you are working on as is tells others you have experience. There are all kinds of ways you can do this without it looking obvious; just be creative and subtle.

Another good strategy is to enlist your male co-workers or supervisors to help you. I've had some awesome male co-workers in my time who noticed when I had to prove myself over and over. Sometimes they noticed this before I did. These types of co-workers can be great in using their own voice and position to talk about your qualifications, experience, expertise, or whatever is needed at a particular moment. And, because they are male their comments are often immediately respected and accepted by all. This is a huge win for you because you didn't have to self-promote yourself but instead earned credibility based on someone else's opinion of you.

And lastly, as with all issues you may be having in the workplace, do take the time to self-evaluate why you may be having to prove yourself over and over again, especially if it's over the same thing. Is your performance falling short or not what it should be? Did you make a mistake the last time and have to earn back respect? Are you trustworthy? As I've stated many times, only you are going to know what is true or not in your performance at work. Don't cheat yourself by ignoring your weaknesses or making the improvements you need make. Don't be afraid to address the obvious. Do it and you will be so much happier with the results.

12

NOT LISTENED TO, NOT UNDERSTOOD, OR TALKED OVER

Not being listened to, understood, and/or being talked over has happened to me so many times over the course of my career—I've honestly lost track. It is very frustrating to be in a work setting and just be ignored, or to contribute to the discussion with no acknowledgment of your contribution, or contributing in a meaningful way and then get cut off or interrupted. Some women I've worked with and coached have described it as feeling invisible.

Like most women, when one of the above happens to me, I automatically assume I said something stupid or inconsequential. And if this happened in a meeting, like most women, I would remain quiet the rest of the meeting because it would shut me down. I had a colleague ask me after a meeting what was wrong because I never said a word. I was floored he didn't see I had been shut down by my supervisor twice for speaking. After thinking about it, he realized this was true and apologized for the situation even though it wasn't his fault.

We have two choices: we can allow ourselves to be shut down or we can get back into the ring.

What would our male counterparts do? If you have ever paid attention in a meeting, men too get shut down. Men don't usually take it so personally. Women immediately internalize criticism and assume it's happening because they have messed up or have no value. Women consider this a sign of their lack of intelligence or ability. Men don't.

I made a huge mistake once by allowing being ignored and shut down to get to me, so much so that I stood up and walked out. As I walked out the door I loudly said to everyone, "When you all feel like being inclusive come get me and I'll happily participate." You could have heard a pin drop. Although it felt good at the time to say what I said, it was actually very unprofessional and made everyone uncomfortable. I was also labeled negatively as not being a team player. I learned a hard lesson.

So what do you do instead? You learn to have patience and breathe deeply to overcome your desire to walk out on everyone or say something you shouldn't.

The first thing is to ask whether or not what is going on is intentional or not. Your strategies are different depending on this answer, so make sure to get it right. You will know it is intentional if someone looks you in the eye and cuts you off or rudely interrupts you.

If unintentional, it is my best advice to continue contributing and stay positive, but persistent. Body language has helped me in this situation a lot. If everyone is sitting, I will stand up and begin talking. This slight shift makes a big difference. And it makes an even bigger difference if I walk up to the whiteboard and grab a marker to illustrate my point. Another trick is to insert yourself as the "summarizer." Start off by summarizing what has been said and maybe even state who said what if it's a smaller group. Then launch into your comment, idea, or contribution. This is a great way to be heard, as people want to hear back to them what they've already said. It's an ego thing where you acknowledge their contribution as a means to get yours in.

Another strategy is to ask a question you don't intend to have really answered, but it makes people stop and think. As they do, you continue on with what you wanted to contribute because you've caught their attention. Obviously this doesn't work with a yes or no question or a rhetorical question. It needs to be a valid question related to the topic at hand, but it is used as your lead in rather than what everyone took it as. For example you could ask, "What if we thought about this a different way?" or "Have you thought about this approach?"

If you are interrupted when you try to contribute, it is also OK to politely say, "I wasn't finished yet." But don't get flustered at having to say those words and then lose your train of thought! Another nice way to say it is, "I see you have something to say too, but let me finish before you do."

Sometimes if your contribution gets no acknowledgment it could be because your thoughts and ideas aren't aligned with the others for whatever reason. Or it could be that you may be a few steps ahead of everyone and you've lost them because they can't catch up with you as quickly. This can happen more often than you would think, especially if you are thinking several steps ahead like women tend to do. Pay attention to the conversation and where people are in their thinking. Continue to ask yourself how your contribution can best help toward the good of the whole. Continue to use communication toward results by saying it another way or with an example, rather than repeating yourself over and over.

My very best tip and a key strategy is to think of yourself as standing or sitting outside of the conversation looking in. This helps you better understand what is motivating people in the conversation, what hot buttons or passions/emotions are driving people to say what they are saying, and how they are responding to each other. Take a look at their body language and see what you can notice. Listen to the tone in their voices, the speed of their words, or anything else to help identify what people are really thinking and feeling inside. Listen for deception, coercion, gameplay, etc. Or listen for excitement, creativity, and innovation. All of this will help you decide how to best engage and have meaningful contributions. Just take thirty seconds to do this. This is, by the way, being purposefully conscious. Being purposefully conscious can be the most valuable method of information gathering you can do in effectively communicating with others.

* * * * *

Intentional behavior to purposely cut you off, ignore your contribution, or talk over you is another animal entirely. We all know people who are mean like this. Remember, the reason most people behave this way is due to their own insecurities and fear. It's highly likely you are being treated in this manner for one or both of these reasons. In my example above where it was my boss who kept cutting me off, it was because of both fear and insecurity. It wasn't readily noticeable, but he was always overcompensating for his lack of self-esteem and fear of people finding out. He had to be "top dog" in all situations—the one with all the answers, the one who made the first move, and the one who directed everyone on what to do next.

So here is what I learned from him and has saved me from many others like him. We all enter the workforce thinking we need to prove ourselves. We need to out-compete our competition. We need to be the person with the best idea. We need to be the one who brought in the biggest client. And mostly this is true. As I've said before, your highest priority is to make your boss look like a superstar. And this is where I failed to realize, instead of competing with him for airtime during a meeting with all my great solutions, I needed to back off and make sure (especially because of his personality) he looked good in front of his peers and subordinates. He kept cutting me off because I was looking smarter than him. As soon as I figured this out, I was able to work my communication towards a more positive end. A simple statement like, "My boss and I came up with this idea …" is an easy way to ensure I was giving him credit, yet I got the airtime to contribute my thoughts. It wasn't a lie as these were ideas we had discussed before, just never acted on. If you can figure out what motivates people to behave the way they do, like why they are ignoring you or cutting you off, you can usually find a way to work around their fear and insecurities.

* * * * *

I'll never forget a man I worked with, a co-worker, who always ignored me and never acknowledged any contribution I made to our team. I asked him in private why, and he simply said, "I just don't like you." I actually chuckled at his statement and said, "Well, fair enough." I thanked him for his honesty and walked away. A funny thing happened after that as he began to ignore me less and less. I teased him in the hallway and said, "You are beginning to like me aren't you?" He didn't answer, but he smiled which was all I needed. I honestly don't think there was an insecurity or fear as the basis for his response toward ignoring me. So sometimes you do encounter people whose behavior isn't fear or insecurity based. I think it was just a plain old personality clash, and yet once we got to know each other, we got along great. It just took some time and patience.

* * * * *

Finally, here is a scene where you are standing in a circle

discussing a topic or issue and find yourself being stood in front of or worked out of the circle somehow. Has this ever happened to you? My husband does this to me on occasion as he will walk over to join a group of us and he'll stand right in front of me. I know he doesn't mean to intentionally or as a sign of disrespect. He, like most men, does it automatically without thinking. It's our job to stop these automatic behaviors and not allow them to happen to us. Especially if we want to be part of this circle and are paid to be part of it.

If you find yourself shut out of a circle or conversation, it is really all about body positioning and body language. You have to establish your place or your spot and stick with it. If someone stands in front of you, you simply saddle up right next to him and re-establish your position. You can even get in his personal space a bit so he has to move over. Sometimes I will stand at a slight angle with my feet hip-distance apart angling toward the person who cut me off or stood in front of me just so I can make eye contact. This eye contact is to make certain he knows you are there and also to show some dominance in the established spot you have made for yourself. It is also necessary to unfold your arms and uncross your legs in order to take up as much physical space as you can. Stand up straight and own your space. If you are short or shorter than all the others, then you really need to use your body positioning and language to best establish yourself.

Once again, it is all about having confidence in yourself and using it. Using your purposeful consciousness to gauge the situation and determine how to effectively navigate through it is also necessary. You have the tools, now just use them.

13

TEARS AT WORK SUCK

Boy do I know an awful lot about tears at work! I admit it: I have cried more times at work than I could count. It seems I cry more easily after having kids too. I'm not sure why that is, but the full-on motherly instinct after having kids is when I noticed a change in my ability to control my tears.

The thing is, I've always been a sensitive person. I cry at commercials on TV, every time the national anthem is played or sung, at parades (I know, parades! What is with that?), and at all kinds of other minor stuff. I also cry whenever I'm in the presence of someone else who is crying. Yep, no one cries alone in my presence! I cry when I am mad and frustrated too.

It is who I am and yet it has never been something I have accepted about myself fully. I accept that I am wired this way, but I am not kind to myself when I cry at things or in places where I don't want to. I honestly hate this about myself—my sensitivity and my quick reaction to cry. Yet, my husband thinks it is one of the best things about me. He has literally never been embarrassed by my crying in public—never. Now that is love!

Most people are surprised by this sensitive side of me as it doesn't show itself often at work, but when it does, it *does!* I genuinely believe people are more accepting of my tears than I am myself. Now isn't that something?

Until about fifteen years ago, I always subscribed to the idea crying at work was a surefire way to give away your power. In my mind, there was just no upside to showing your emotions and crying. I think most people feel this way. As a woman, I just never wanted to give men another reason to look down on us or criticize us for being "too emotional." My thoughts on crying at work have changed over the years but for good reason and for the better too.

Generally, I do think it's the best idea to not let your emotions get the best of you at work. Crying uncontrollably at work over something minor is definitely not good. But I think it's quite acceptable to shed a tear or two with people you trust at work over work-related issues or personal issues, especially if it is for just for a few moments.

It is also acceptable to cry for reasons or experiences shared by others such as the passing of a fellow employee, the diagnosis of a colleague's devastating illness, a tragic accident of a co-worker's child, or something along these lines. Sometimes there is comfort in sharing tears with one another to acknowledge the pain and sort through the emotions everyone is feeling.

We have to be allowed to be human, even at work. Yet its always a good idea if you are about to break down to take a walk outside or find a nearby bathroom to cry, collect yourself, and take a deep breath. You aren't always going to have this opportunity, but when you do you should take advantage of it. There are going to be times when you cry in front of others too.

When you do cry at work (notice I didn't say "if," because it's likely to happen), it's important to acknowledge what is making you feel this emotion so strongly it created tears. And when I say, "acknowledge," I mean to name it. You need to name the circumstance, the memory, the way you are being treated, the anger, or whatever it may be. Name it so you can address and deal with whatever is bothering you. You may need to talk it out with a friend or loved one after work. Maybe you need to spend time alone to work through your emotions to get to a place of peace, acceptance, or whatever is needed. Your job, when you have emotions that cause you to cry in public, is to do what is needed to take care of you.

How many of you have apologized after you have cried? We feel like we need to excuse our behavior or we feel ashamed and have to apologize for it. Apologizing can actually make those around you feel more uncomfortable, which is the opposite of what you want. When you apologize you also draw more attention to yourself, which isn't what you desire either. And lastly, apologies often make you cry more or worse. I just gave you three reasons not to apologize for your tears. Don't do it! Just move on and others around you will likely move on with you. The worst thing people can do when I am in tears is hug me, console me, tell me "you poor thing," and make a big deal about it. It makes it worse! So don't make a big deal of it yourself either. And for heaven's sake, do the same for others when you are on the receiving end of tears. I just want to be left alone to gather myself and move on. So respect others by doing the same.

In all my years of working and supervising women, it seems the main reason for tears in the workplace is when you have been pushed to an unfamiliar or uncomfortable place where you are left feeling helpless, vulnerable, and powerless. By and large, when you name the circumstance or emotions causing you to cry, it will be tied to these feelings in some way. The good thing is, crying can actually help you to deal with these emotions so you can think clearly and focus on solutions to feeling vulnerable or helpless. That is the end goal after all: to work through this unfamiliar or uncomfortable place to one that familiar and comfortable.

* * * * *

As a leader and supervisor in my organization, my tears had some positive benefits too. Tears told people how I really felt deep down inside. Tears spoke volumes about how deeply invested I was. And they also showed how much my work meant to me. People saw the real me, the raw emotion of who I was. And in this sense, my tears were a very powerful way of communicating. Tears can express a vulnerability and authenticity that strengthens rather than diminishes us in the eyes of our co-workers.

I once had an employee who said my tears were tears of strength and I'll never forget how his words touched me so. He was right; I could still direct a mission with tears in my eyes and flowing down my cheeks. Because of how I am wired, I had to learn not to run and hide every time I cried. If I did, I wouldn't have gotten much work done.

I cry when I am angry and I have often had to tell others, "I am crying because I am angry. This is what it looks like when I am pissed." And then I continue on as if I didn't have a face full of tears.

I had to lead some really difficult times at work with tears and tissues. I have stood in front of hundreds of firefighters with tears and yet clearly communicated how I wanted the day to progress and people to work together safely despite the loss the day before. I've had to give a eulogy at an employee's memorial service with tears and tissues. I've had to deliver very difficult news to my employees and community with misty eyes.

Tears, as a sign of strength, can increase your ability to lead people if you are able to confidently stand without fear of your own outpouring of emotion.

I think this bolded statement is the lesson to be learned and the place you need to work on getting to if you are at all a person who has or will cry at work. Don't apologize. Own your emotions, stand confidently, and move on.

14

BEING FEMALE MEANS I'M NOT SMART ENOUGH OR STRONG ENOUGH? GIVE ME A BREAK!

I was never more embarrassed in all of my career over being physically weak than when I couldn't change a flat tire on my work-assigned truck. I had spent the entire day working in the forest on my own, getting a lot done and enjoying the day. I came back to my truck to find I had a flat tire, which is common in my line of work as a forester. However, on this day with this particular tire, I couldn't get the lug nuts off for the life of me. I tried every trick there was! I probably spent over an hour and could not get one lug nut off—not one! I was so angry I almost cried.

Unfortunately, I had only one choice and that was to call using the radio to my office and ask for help. Calling on the radio meant everyone would hear me too. I would have rather died a thousand deaths than have EVERYONE know I was helpless. Yet, I was stuck with no other option as there was no cell service and I couldn't wait all afternoon and evening hoping someone might come by. Besides, I was a long way back in the woods so the odds of someone coming by were pretty low.

I mustered up all the guts I had and made the call. An hour later I had help. And although no negative words came from his mouth about being a helpless female or not being strong enough to take care of the job, I just knew he had to be thinking what I was thinking. But he was nice, and he was nice enough to also make a point about how hard it was for him to get those lug nuts off too. And they were; he struggled and struggled (even with my "help").

Back at the office, I didn't receive any teasing or snide comments. Overall, I was definitely harder on myself than anyone else was. Yet, I couldn't help thinking I had let myself look weak in front of everyone. I couldn't help thinking I was letting down my fellow women too.

Every flat tire from that point forward I made a point of changing, regardless of how many people I was with or how many males I was with. It was like I had to prove to everyone, "See, I can do this."

Many years later I was driving with the under sheriff and a deputy. We had a forest fire and were evaluating the need for evacuations, so the three of us were surveying the situation. Lo and behold, we got a flat tire.

I was on it. It wasn't my vehicle, but it didn't matter. I was not going to let these two male law enforcement officers see that I couldn't hold my own. After getting started and making it happen, the under sheriff got to the point where he and the deputy just stood back and watched. They couldn't get over how funny it was to have me changing their tire for them. Soon enough, the under sheriff got out his video camera and tried to catch the whole thing on tape (this was before smartphones). I was beaming inside and out. I finally felt like I had been vindicated.

Of course back at the office, the two officers had to laugh it up with anyone who would listen. The video camera, it turns out, didn't have a charged battery so there was no proof, just a funny story.

What I forgot and got fixated on due to one flat tire is the fact that being mentally strong and physically tough is almost entirely a state of mind. It is sad how I let one flat tire get me down like it did. I was the one who made my inability to change it a big deal in my mind; it wasn't any of my co-workers.

I'm guessing this happens all too often where we internalize an event and make it into the end of the world when it never felt or seemed that way to anyone else. How many of you have said something really stupid in front of your peers or supervisors/managers and walked away with your head in your hands and feeling like life as you knew it was over? I know I have.

* * * * *

Our abilities are often judged solely by our gender. I know this to be the case as I too have lived it as well. We all know employees who cannot accept the idea of women who are strong and can work hard. We also know people who believe women are inferior in certain fields such as science, technology, engineering, and math because we simply are not smart enough or our brains aren't wired to be successful in these fields.

I get it; it's a decades-old story about women not being strong enough, tough enough, or smart enough. Unfortunately, this attitude is still present in today's workplace. Yet this attitude and culture are slowly changing too. We just need to give it a bigger push and here's how.

I told you we aren't going to blame men, society, culture, or the past. Yes, these all need to change for the better and for the benefit of women everywhere. However, let's start with the change in ourselves first. Let it take root and grow.

* * * * *

Here's the next big secret I am going to share with you in this book. It's another breakthrough.

Your strength and your intelligence are most certainly and almost entirely a state of mind.

Have you ever heard of grit? Mental toughness is commonly called "grit." I use them interchangeably. For me, grit is defined as your perseverance and passion combined together towards achieving a long-term goal.

Why is it some people succeed and others don't? Believe it or not, your talent, your physical strength, and your intelligence do not play as big of a role in your success as you might think. And there are studies that prove this to be true, which I won't cite here but you can do an Internet search if you wish.

If grit is a state of mind, then it doesn't matter what naysayers think or say. They are just noise. What does matter is your own state of mind and keeping it focused on achieving your long-term goal or goals using your mental toughness. It's more than just one flat tire!

All I can say is, thank goodness talent is overrated. Grit is what makes us successful in work and in overall life. Grit can be what we are known for and what we are respected for. I don't know about you, but I would much rather be defined by my passion and perseverance than over my lack of ability to run a mile in less than eight minutes or be able to score in the top ten percent on my college SATs.

We are all going to get knocked down from time to time due to people and circumstances causing us to feel inferior, inadequate, or stupid. The mental toughness kicks in when we choose not to let it knock us down or keep us knocked down. Here is where being purposefully conscious can help us be more consistent with our grit and likely develop levels of grit above what we thought were even possible.

Where does grit come from? Again, it's a state of mind, but it is also something that needs to be expressed as tangible actions. I say "actions" as plural because these actions need to happen every day of your life. For example, you can't just envision being able to land the biggest account in company history. You have to work at this daily, making small gains toward this goal, which may include making and learning from mistakes along the way. You have to push yourself as you grow and develop on your path toward long-term success. Your small victories and accomplishments along the way will test you. This means when the big time comes you will be ready when things get really difficult, and you will accomplish what you set out to do.

We see grit played out on our favorite television show all the time by the heroine or hero who saves the day, solves the case, or saves a life. It took grit to get through medical school and all the training to become the doctor who saves lives. It was small and tangible actions of grit to study hard for each test, practice using the instruments and tools of the trade, and making it through long shifts as an intern. A first-year pre-med student wasn't capable of performing the life-saving operation overnight, but when it was time to do so years and years later the small tangible successes or "wins" paid off.

Grit isn't willpower. Grit isn't even motivation. Grit comes from someplace much deeper inside. It's being inspired. It's the kind of inspiration that lights up every fiber in your being. It's the passion that carries you to overcome and outlast any short-term obstacle or distraction. And lastly, it's about the consistency and courage to remain focused and follow-through.

Do you have grit, the kind that I speak of? Do you want it? I'm telling you, this mental toughness is a powerful thing in your abilities to achieve your goals.

If you want it, it's totally within you to create it.

Determine what your long-term goal is and who you need to be to achieve it. Who are you and what is your identity when you tackle those short-term actions leading you closer to your long-term goal? What habits or behaviors do you need to develop in tackling these short-term actions? Maybe this is done through a routine or a schedule to keep you on track. Use whatever method you need to ensure the tracks you are laying are gaining you ground.

Remember, you don't have to be excellent at every single thing asked of you at work. For example, when I was fighting fire I was a beast at chopping trees with an ax, digging fire line, hiking as well as any of the guys, and even running a chainsaw. But I wasn't good when I was loaded down with fifty extra pounds of fire hose or water to carry up a mountain. I slowed way down. But here's the thing, I was good at the majority of the work involved in fire fighting. When I couldn't keep up after adding fifty pounds of gear on my back, the men on the crew never made fun of me or thought less of me. They saw me work day after day for sixteen hours as hard as I could giving 110% and this is what they valued: someone they could count on to be mentally tough, physically able, and willing to joke when a good laugh was needed. You don't have to rock out every single task, just be really good at the majority of them and recognize there are going to be a few physical limitations we can't overcompensate for. We are allowed to be human, and men understand this too. No one expects a superhero.

In the end, don't let the joke be on you by limiting yourself or believing you are not being capable of doing a job because you don't feel smart enough or physically strong enough. Mental toughness and grit are how success is measured, so the joke is certainly on anyone who doubts a woman who has it.

15

I'M TIRED OF BEING CALLED
THE DIVERSITY HIRE

My first permanent job in natural resource management was met with these words, "You were only hired because you are female." Truth is, they were probably right. At that time, more females were being hired than males, especially in professional positions like mine.

But what most didn't know, unlike the other females hired at the same time, is that I actually had years of work experience. Most of the other females had never worked in natural resource management before. I had put in three summers already before starting college and had fought fire too. Let's just say my employer got a pretty good bang for their buck when they hired me!

So when people would tell me I was only hired because I was female, because I knew it to be true, I'd respond with, "Yes, that's true. But I'm a female with more experience than you." Or I would just say, "Yes, that's true. But I have a whole lot more going for me than that."

It appeared to me the "hired because you are female" comment made it once around the office and then stopped. I wasn't ever called a diversity hire again. I did two things right at the young age of twenty when I didn't know better. I acknowledged the comment and didn't let it get my goat. And I also did a little self-promotion which might not have been so modest, but it was effective.

Are you a diversity hire? If you are, so what? Who cares if you had a leg up on everyone else because of your gender or ethnicity? People get hired for all kinds of different reasons. The guy hired next to you might have been selected because he was friends with the hiring manager, so don't tell me he didn't have a leg up.

When you are being targeted with comments such as being called the diversity hire, you certainly can ignore it and go on with doing the fabulous job you are doing. This isn't a bad approach, because over time people will quit talking badly about you. It's true, it will go away.

* * * * *

People act out with negative comments like this for two reasons. The first is because they are jealous you got the job over them or someone they know. And second, they are doing it just to test you and see what your reaction will be. Knowing which reason isn't critical to know, but sometimes it is helpful.

There have been several times in my career where I've gotten a job over someone else and then I ended up having to work with that person. This is never an easy situation and one you may not know going into the job. You might find out days or months later. Either way, I have always found it helpful to address the situation. I've always talked to the individual I beat out for the job in a one-on-one setting. I make sure to tell them I know they put in for the job and explain it is not my intention to make it more uncomfortable for them than it already is. Most importantly, I treat this person with respect, particularly for the positive attributes they do have and contribute. In every situation, the person has responded with appreciation for being sensitive to the situation and the empathy I have in them not getting the job they competed for. Because I do this very important act of kindness and respect, I have rarely had a problem getting along and working with the individual. In the one case where I did, it was because this person saw to it that everything was a competition. My approach then quickly changed to how I could support this individual and help them in furthering their career with everything I had in my power to do. Once they realized my support was genuine, our relationship improved immediately.

I have found it harder to deal with someone who had a friend who they believed deserved the job over me. This is harder to work through because they feel it is a loyalty issue if they decide to support or befriend me. This situation just takes time and patience and then more time and patience. There really isn't much you can or should do in this situation, because you do not want to get in the middle. It's too risky and not worth it.

For those individuals who say negative or even discriminatory statements to you just to see if they can get a rise out of you, consider this as a test of your character and a chance for you to show others you are professional. Don't let it bother you one iota, because this is exactly what they want. They want it to affect you by either making you mad or shaking your confidence. Don't let it. Remember, you choose your response to situations. Don't let others choose your response for you. You are being set up, and the only way to get them to back down and quit is to remain a professional. As an example, you might say something like I did in my story at the beginning of the chapter. Or you could say, "Well I'm here now, despite why I was hired." And then follow with a comment about last night's game or with a question to quickly change the topic and divert everyone's attention away from you. These tactics work quite well.

Figure out what your one-liner is going to be, and it would be great if this one-liner also does double duty as a means to keep the "you were only hired because you are a female" comment from coming up again and again.

Stay cool. This too will pass, especially if you work on the other things in this book to become the exceptional employee and leader you were hired to be.

16

WOMEN CAN'T BE GOOD MANAGERS BECAUSE THEY ARE TOO EMOTIONAL

I have been told by several male managers as I began my career that women aren't able to "cut it" at the upper levels of the organization because their emotions get in the way. I've also been told women can't be good managers because we are "too soft," "easily manipulated," and "lack the ability to make the tough decisions." I don't know about you, but this gets old real quick.

There is no question I am an emotional person, and I do wear my emotions on my sleeve most of the time. I've coined a term for myself; I'm "empathetically blunt." I have compassion and understanding for people and situations, yet when it comes down to it I will be pretty darned blunt in my response to it. I think this is why people are surprised when I cry easily, which is the soft and empathetic side of my personality many aren't used to seeing. On the other hand, friends and family are surprised to see the sure-footed leader I can be.

That is how I am built; each of us are extremely complex beings in our personalities at home, at work, and in social settings. Our complexity increases when we experience stress and major life events too.

In some ways it is true that if you are an emotional mess and can't think or function well, you will not be a good leader or manager. But being emotional is not the predictor of your ability or failure. And certainly, just because you are a woman doesn't mean anything either.

Most of the information and scientific studies I have read suggests emotional intelligence is a better predictor of success.

Regardless of what is going on in our world, those with emotional intelligence tend to be better equipped to handle it.

What is this thing called emotional intelligence? In simple language, it includes self-awareness, management of emotions, empathy, and social skills.

I talked about self-awareness earlier in this book, but called it "purposeful consciousness" which is equivalent to the kind of self-awareness used to describe emotional intelligence.

When you hear the phrase "management of emotions," you might immediately think you aren't very good at it. But think about it for a minute because you may be better at it than you give yourself credit for. Do you lash out at co-workers when they have made a mistake causing you more work? Do you yell at others? Do you blame others to cover up your mistakes? If you said no to these questions, then you might be showing some emotional intelligence.

Instead of telling the boss how you really think, do you express your feelings instead with careful control and toward a positive outcome? Do you show restraint in holding back anger or frustration? Do you use your judgment and control in expressing your emotions? If you answered yes to any of these questions, you should give yourself some credit. Many of us can always use improvement with being more emotionally intelligent. If you know this to be true about yourself, you are showing self-awareness. Make sure your "management of emotions" isn't so extreme where you are suppressing every emotion or thought. It is OK to express your emotions and thoughts, but do so in a manner that is constructive, professional, and with a high level of good judgment.

Empathy isn't about giving people an easy out or not holding them accountable. Empathy is our emotional ability to connect with others, to have understanding for one another, and to have compassion too. And lastly, your social skills are what build trust with others. Your excellent social skills also help you to bring out the best in people as well as increase your ability to connect and sync with teams.

You aren't born with emotional intelligence, but it's something gained throughout your life if you choose to learn and apply it. And despite what you may think, women aren't necessarily better at it than men either.

What is true is that the higher up in an organization you go, especially with more supervision and leadership responsibilities, the more important emotional intelligence is to be successful. Emotional intelligence also gives those who have it an edge in the workplace. Positions in sales, being on teams, leading teams, and overall leadership is where emotional intelligence is most needed and recognized.

I'm not hung up on emotional intelligence being the greatest thing ever. In fact, I think the key point is taking everything you've learned in this book and putting it all together (which includes self-awareness, managing emotions, empathy, and social skills) toward a more successful you. Who cares if it is called emotional intelligence or not?

Your success is about being able to work all the attributes you have in a positive and meaningful way toward achieving the results you want in your life.

This bolded statement is your take-home message. This is what will make a difference in your life if you choose to do so.

If I had to boil it down even further, I'd suggest what is vitally important in today's global economy and marketplace is your critical thinking and communication skills. In essence, your ability to increase the energy of others in problem solving, creative thinking, strategic planning, or whatever the work demands at the time is the true skill. This means you aren't necessarily trying to be the "golden girl" sweeping in with all the answers and saving the day.

Leverage your skills and contribution toward a greater good and value. Use your attributes towards a larger mission as a team in a way that builds everyone to a greater capacity.

This isn't easy to do and requires you to be excellent at listening, understanding others, communicating so you are understood, and in engaging others. This does require you to put your ego aside too. And it requires patience.

For me, being a good listener was always a struggle. There is no doubt I spent more time as a manager thinking ahead of everyone else rather than sitting back and being patient enough to just listen. This was something I had to learn to do better, which for me meant I needed to slow down. It also meant I had to control the urge to interrupt people, which is a huge dead give away to others you are not listening to them. Listening is a skill. For me, it's more about being purposefully conscious than anything. I can be a great listener, I just have to consciously make the choice to physically and mentally do so.

Being self-aware is an essential component to emotional intelligence. Being self-aware provides you with the ability to make choices with regard to managing your emotions, having empathy, and using your social skills. If you are running on autopilot and in your unconscious mode of automatic behaviors, you aren't in a good space. Our unconscious motivations, bias, and beliefs can have a negative impact on our ability to be effective employees, managers, and leaders if we choose to ignore them and let them play out in the workplace. And lastly, the ability for us to use our self-awareness as a tool to listen to feedback on our own performance (both positive and negative) is essential in today's workforce. This shows maturity and humility in our growth as a person by being willing to accept we are not perfect but are working on ourselves to be better each and every day.

* * * * *

There are many people who believe careers and jobs in science, technology, engineering, and math will mean they won't have to work with people. I know I hear this a lot in my profession where people took jobs in natural resource management because they thought they would just be working in the forest by themselves alone. This is the biggest misunderstanding there is in today's working world. There are so few fields in today's workplace where you work alone, aren't assigned to a team or teams, or aren't asked to work with customers or clients. And thus, the measure for success in today's workplace isn't your gender, the amount of emotions you have, your education, or your intelligence. I hope you see now how your success is driven by your aptitude in the areas discussed in this chapter and throughout this book. True self-awareness and work in these areas will improve your life beyond the working environment too, which is a tremendous benefit and motivation as well.

17

I'M CONVINCED IF I START A FAMILY, MY CAREER WILL END

It weighs heavy on my heart to hear women speak about the dilemma of, "Can I have a career and be a mom?" Your decision to start a family is the biggest decision you'll ever make, regardless of your profession.

What I can share with you is the challenge I faced raising babies and being a career woman and how I worked through the challenges in hopes it will help you see yourself succeed as both a working woman and mother.

What kind of mother are you? – As a new mother preparing to go back to work, I remember how hard it was for me to incorporate my new role and go back to my old one. Seriously, this was extremely difficult for me and a brain bender. I was asked to come back to work early from my maternity leave, so I didn't have a lot of time to process it either. It wasn't until I stopped in to visit the daycare center I would soon be using for my son that it all hit me like a ton of bricks. I cried and cried when I left, not being able to believe I was the type of person who could leave my nearly newborn child with someone else. Was I an awful person to even consider it? But here is the thing, I was creating negative self-talk by telling myself I was a bad mother and person for wanting to go back to work. How many women do this to ourselves when we are at the crossroads of work and motherhood?

I am not a bad mother and was not a bad person for making the choice to leave my son at daycare and go back to work. After getting very honest with myself, I knew I did not have the right personality to be a stay-at-home mom. I knew I had goals I wanted to achieve at work, promotions I wanted to try for, and a career I wanted to pursue. I had to allow myself to accept who I was inside. I was a working mother and there was certainly no need for the negative self-talk and doubt. I admire stay-at-home mothers and I thought I could be one, but I found out otherwise. Getting to know this about myself was in some ways very freeing. I was able to get over the guilt and be free to like myself for who I was in my new role as a working mother. The ah-ha moment was, if I wasn't true to myself, then I couldn't be true to anyone else in my life. If I wasn't true to myself, how could I be the mother I am meant to be? The last thing I wanted was to resent my decision, and to this day I have not.

Motherhood changes you. It *should* change you. But you need to be confident in who you are and what you want in your new role. If that is being a career woman, then you need to stay true to that person. If that means your career isn't a priority anymore, then accept this and move on to what is. If that means staying home with your children is your priority, that's great too.

I've supervised and seen a lot of young women in my time who have had entry-level positions and been very good at their jobs. Entry-level positions, in natural resource management, generally means you work primarily outdoors. For some reason I still can't quite understand how after having a baby these women suddenly "don't" or "can't" work outdoors. I would see them making excuses for having too much "office work" to do or "the baby wasn't feeling well when I dropped her off at daycare, and I don't want to get too far away from the office" or "I'm still nursing or pumping." The excuses would go on and on. I was always stunned by this phenomenon, which I truly felt was a phenomenon.

Maybe the reason I have never understood this is because this didn't happen to me. I suppose I made sure it didn't because I didn't want to look like or act like these other new mothers. In fact, while I was pregnant with my second child there was an office poll as to where I would drop and have this kid while working in the woods. The baby in my belly hiked a lot of miles in the mountains working on projects. I had my firstborn in daycare while I carried my second child, and I always knew if he got sick, even if I wasn't in cell reception, my office would call me on the radio and tell me to come back in. After having each child, I pumped my milk at work religiously. I even bought a vehicle adapter for my pump so I could pump while I was working in the outdoors. You find ways to make it work and not use your kids or motherhood as an excuse. Using your kids is a terrible excuse and everyone can see through it. You aren't fooling anyone but yourself. You can make being a working mother work for you, but you have to be determined to do so and make conscious choices.

Again, if being a new mother has changed you and changed your goals in life and at work, then be honest with yourself about it and be proud of it too. Look for ways to make the career changes you need to make and act. Don't live a lie when you aren't the same person anymore. You are a woman and a mother, which gives you the right to make the best decisions for you.

Find your village – Once you are confident you are a working mother, you are going to need to be OK with leaving your kiddos.

Trust me, this is easier said than done. Your confidence in who you are and why you are pushing your career forward is critical. Some people will understand what you are doing and why, and others won't. If you have the confidence about who you are, you will rise above this noise and do what you were meant to do for yourself.

Fathers leave their children with their wife and family all the time and it's accepted. Why is this the opposite for women? Our culture and our societal norms of men being the breadwinners are the reason for this. I would say that if the father of your children is supportive of your career and is willing to play a major role in raising his family, then you have the makings for success. There is nothing wrong with leaving your children in the capable hands of their father. And better yet, if you have other friends and family who can support him and help out as needed, you certainly have no reason to be worried.

The demands of the district manager job required me to leave my kids a lot. There is nothing wrong with leaving your kids in the loving hands of a friend, family member, or father. It really is good for all involved. It's because of work trips and special assignments that my kids have formed some special bonds with their dad. It's because of my work absences that my kids have learned to stay overnight at grandma's house without their parents. We mothers feel like it's a terrible tragedy to leave our kids when it's not. Never feel guilty when you've got a tribe or village to help you out. In fact, take advantage of it when you need to. If you don't have a village, start creating one.

It gets easier at the top – The higher up you go, the more autonomy you have. Lower graded positions are generally less flexible, have tighter supervision, and require you to be physically located at the workplace. If you are on a career track, you need to realize this. For me in my career, I looked at it as a short-term sacrifice for a long-term gain. This became a reality for me when I got the call to take the temporary promotion in a district manager position a few months after my second child was born. This temporary promotion was located five hours from our home, and it was in a small town where there was no daycare.

After long discussions with my husband and my "village," we decided the best thing to do was to leave my two-year-old son with my husband where my son would have the least disruption to his home and daycare. My two-month-old daughter would come with me since I was still nursing her, and my mother and mother-in-law would trade off each week staying with us in the location of my temporary assignment. This decision was so difficult. I cried and cried the day I left my son. I let my mind play games with me again. All I heard from my negative self-talk was what a terrible mother I was for leaving my son for my career. However, I knew if I could succeed in this assignment this would all be to our benefit. I kept reminding myself of this over and over again.

My husband was a complete champ as he too wanted what we both knew lay ahead for my career. I came home every weekend except for one when my son was so sick we decided it was best for the baby and I to stay away. What I saw over time was the relationship between my husband and son getting stronger. They bonded and became buddies. My son had been a "mama's boy" up to that point, and he definitely changed into an independent little man I was so proud of. This bonding was really good for them. And my mother and mother-in-law both had a ball trading off being "nanny." My "village" was happy to serve when they were needed and to support their kids as we made moves toward bettering our careers.

After being a district manager for a few years, the autonomy of the position really began, and I found myself leaving meetings early to pick the kids up from school or to attend their ball games. I would ask one of my employees to take a meeting for me so I wouldn't have to go out of town. I also flexed my schedule to do what was needed of my demanding job yet be there for my family. The position afforded me this; for that I was grateful, and it certainly made it easier for me to be the person I wanted to be wearing all the hats I wore.

I appreciated being in a leadership role where I modeled the work-life balance I wanted my employees to also have. When they saw me leave at 4:00 p.m. to pick up my kids from school and go straight home, this sent a positive message. When I took sick days to stay home with sick kids, this too sent a message. I looked at it as a way to change the culture at work, modeling the behavior I wanted to see in others.

I learned that it's all about quality, not quantity. Quality time with my kids when I didn't have much time meant the household chores could wait, supper could be from the microwave, etc.

The only thing our kids want from us is us. So when quality time really mattered, my phone would be put away and other distractions held to a minimum. The best quality time was getting on the floor and playing, reading, and playing some more. It was about cuddles and nap times together too.

Another secret I will share with you is to speak about your family obligations as "appointments." If it was nearing 4:00 p.m. and I was on the phone with someone or in a meeting, I would excuse myself by saying I had another appointment to get to. And I did; I had a very important appointment to pick up my kids from school on time. If my kids had an away basketball game where I needed to be gone for most of the afternoon, I would block out my schedule with it as an appointment. If someone wanted to schedule something during that time, I would say I have a conflict in my schedule with another appointment. Most people hear the word "appointment" and think you mean something work related. Rarely have I been asked what kind of appointment.

In summary, it is clear there are no right answers. Only you hold the answers that are right for you. Do some soul searching and start out with the big one—the type of mother you are and want to be. After you know this, which again, may not be until after you have a family, do what it takes to be true to you. This in turn will result in you being the best person you can be for your children, your spouse, your village, and your work.

18

WORK-LIFE BALANCE: IS IT A DREAM OR IS IT A NIGHTMARE?

Work-life balance is a tough deal and many people don't do well with it at all. In fact, I could write a whole book on how to achieve work-life balance, and I will likely do that one day. In the meantime, I will share with you a few secrets I have on how I achieved it and made it work for me.

Work-life balance is a continual evaluation, assessment, and adjustment process.

Work-life balance isn't something you achieve and then you are good to go for years to come. Unfortunately, it just doesn't work that way. And there is no such thing as "perfect" work-life balance, so just get rid of the word "perfect" as it has no place in our conversation about this topic!

Just say no – I hate to break this to you, but you really can't do it all. Don't kid yourself thinking you can. You really need to say "no" to some things in your life, which means you are going to have to say "no" to people. It never feels good to say "no," but for your own sanity and your own balance, you need to do so. Saying "no" does get easier over time. The first couple out of your mouth are the toughest. And after you say "no," make sure you keep the commitment to yourself. Also, make sure you don't put yourself on a guilt trip either. You aren't going to make everyone happy, but if people are worth having in your life, you will know by how they are willing to accept your "no."

At work when you say "no," you do need to make sure it is something you can say "no" to. If it is your job, you really can't say "no" sometimes. But you can ask for time off, flexible time, or to be removed from a special committee assignment not related to your job. You don't have to be the person at work who plans every holiday party or potluck. You don't have to be the person who cleans the kitchen/break room each evening. You don't have to be the chair of the welcoming committee. You don't have to accept every invitation by your co-workers to go out for lunch when you really need to run a few errands or exercise instead. Some people react negatively if you aren't a "joiner," but they will get over it and you just need to stick to doing what is best for you.

Prioritize, organize, and prioritize again – I have learned to get anything done, including downtime, you have to prioritize. I prioritize everything in my life, so much so that it's second nature. I even prioritize household chores, which seems overboard, but it is effective. Such as, just because my best-looking jeans or favorite shirt are dirty, do I really need to do a load of laundry? Maybe I just need to wear some of the other clothes in my closet and let them have some fun too. I recently realized my favorite three pairs of socks were the only ones I was wearing and after three days, I'd do a load of laundry. How silly! I bought four more pairs just like them and now I can go a full week without doing a load. Talk about time savings! I prioritize whether I should clean my microwave or not. I consider if I will be having company soon or not and put off the cleaning until I do. Prioritizing at its finest ladies!

Down time for relaxing, meditation, and exercising also has to be prioritized. If you don't prioritize it in your schedule, it will likely not happen because we all short-change ourselves when it comes to "me time." This is the first thing to go when we get busy, stressed, or overworked. We value ourselves and our time to recharge our batteries less than we value keeping up with everything else. And if you think about it, this is backward from the way it should be. We should be making sure our batteries are fully charged so we can tackle the rest. But we don't. We'd rather work on an empty tank which increases our chances of making mistakes, forgetting something, not doing tasks well, being tired and dragging our butts, and making poor decisions. This doesn't make sense. If you want to operate at top performance, then you need to schedule in and prioritize your down time.

There are a number of activities that suck the majority of our time away too. For me that is Facebook. I'm not sure why I feel compelled to keep up with everyone's statuses. Life won't end if I don't keep up with my news feed. Watch for the time suckers in your own world and make sure you are deliberate in how much time you give them. If you find you are starting to spend more time on them than you had planned, then stop and go to the items on your to-do list that are a higher priority. Don't give the time suckers control over your precious time.

I think the key to this prioritization is to get to a point where you aren't just putting out fires all the time and running from urgent tasks to urgent tasks. To do this, you need to plan ahead and anticipate. This doesn't mean there won't be urgent matters that come up from time to time, yet many can be avoided with planning. It's also important to work on tasks along the way to avoid the situation of them becoming urgent. Balance can be much easier to achieve if you aren't constantly chasing urgent tasks. And you will have more energy if you are planning ahead, rather than the urgent matters causing extra stress and draining you.

A modified unplug – We have all heard we should "unplug" (turn off our phone, computers, and other devices) to better attain work-life balance. And you have most likely thought, "Oh, I can't do that" for one reason or another. Guess what, you can. Even if you are tied to your phone or other device twenty-four seven due to the duties of your job or because you have a personal need to be notified for something important, you can do a modified "unplug."

This is what I do: I will stay plugged in but will only react to the notifications needing immediate attention. I am often carrying my smartphone around with me in the evening, but only to get a text from my kids of when I need to pick them up from practice. I won't read or respond to work e-mails, LinkedIn connection requests, Facebook notifications, etc. This takes dedication and commitment on your part, but you can honor yourself and keep yourself in check to practice this. I feel quite content with a modified unplug because it allows me to know what is going on, but it doesn't mean I have to respond to it. Not knowing what is going on at all stresses me out more than the energy it takes to be dedicated to a modified "unplug."

Exercise or wellness activity – I don't care what type of activity you choose, getting into a habit of regular exercise and wellness is tremendous in helping to find and maintain your work-life balance. My typical choices are power walking, running, lifting weights, and yoga. I have something wrong with my back causing me issues from time to time, so my yoga practice is essential in alleviating pain and allowing me to feel human. By far, my favorite activity is power walking, and I always take my dog with me. I walk a very brisk four-miles-per-hour pace on the roads around our home, which have a lot of hills, so I definitely get a good workout. What I love about my power walks is what it does for my attitude and brain. Not only do I feel refreshed, but I often come back having solved problems. I often come up with new or creative ideas, mentally organize and prioritize my to-do list, remember things I forgot, and more. These walks are almost the most important thing I can do each day. Because of this, I highly recommend finding your go-to activity as a surefire way to improve the balance in your life.

Be who you are – I just never was someone who didn't wear all my hats at all times. At work, I was never able to not talk about my kids or about stuff going on in my personal life. I enjoyed knowing about the children and grandchildren of my co-workers and employees and certainly never hesitated to ask questions and to be interested. When at work or when off, I am always the whole woman. I was never someone who separated being a mother and being a career woman. For me, this is a matter of balance in my life and in who I am as a person.

During the same fire event I spoke about at the very beginning of the book, I conducted public meetings every night to make sure I was keeping the community informed. These meetings were very popular and during the height of the fire activity and were attended by 250 – 500 people. One evening the governor even attended. At these meetings, I would have a microphone and would share information about the day's events concerning the fire, the strategies and tactics we were using, and anything else that was of importance. After several days of meetings, community leaders and even the local pastors became part of the meeting. These meetings became the community's meetings and were a gathering where families and neighbors came together to support each other and the fire suppression efforts. The microphone was shared with our local sheriff, local fire department chief, and our state fire partners. These meetings were tremendous in our ability to work effectively with the public and people were grateful for them.

My mom was staying with us during the fire to help out with the kids who were nine months and two years old at the time. She would bring the kids to the meeting and pack a picnic supper for us to eat after the meeting together as a family. Working sixteen hours a day, this time with my family was very valuable especially when my husband was able to join us too.

One night before the meeting I had a few moments to visit with my mom. She told me that my daughter, who was nine months old at the time, had taken her first tentative steps to walk earlier in the day. I was so excited. The meeting began, and I was doing my thing up in front of everyone talking about the day's fire activity when I noticed something in the back of the crowd. It was my daughter, and she was determined to walk up to me. As she did, everyone noticed where my attention had gone because that girl stopped me right in mid-sentence. She was walking! Tears began to flow down my cheeks as I paused and waited for her to walk up to me. I picked her up in my arms and told her how proud I was of her, then wiped away my tears and addressed the crowd again. The fire had been stressful for everyone in the community, and I explained these were my daughter's first steps everyone just got to see. I went on to say how important it was during this time of stress to remember the little things and to take care of each other. Seeing a child's first steps were a reminder to us all to remember what is most important in life.

After every meeting I was usually flooded with people who wanted to talk more or ask questions. After that night, I didn't think I'd ever get done talking one-on-one with people. The reaction to my daughter's first steps and my tears were profound, and people were moved by it. It was a connection with my community that was valuable in gaining trust and in being more than just a "talking head." Being new to the job by only a few months, these public meetings were valuable for the community in being able to see me for who I was as a person which included being a wife, mother, and district manager. The whole woman revealed.

19

BULLYING & SEXUAL HARASSMENT IS A BIG DEAL

If you feel you are being bullied or sexually harassed at work, you need to seek out professional advice and help. I am not that source for you; you need to find someone who is. You need to understand the policies at your workplace, assuming your workplace has them, and if they do not, this should be a red flag. You need to understand your rights and responsibilities. You need to put the bullying or harassment in writing, even if you don't ever disclose it to your employer, particularly if you ever decide to file a claim or create a case.

Quite simply, sexual harassment is against the law. For most companies discrimination may also be a violation of our nation's laws protecting our civil rights. Many companies may also have additional policies to regulate hostile working environments as well.

I will say, I am truly sorry if you find yourself in this situation. Your circumstance will likely challenge and test you unlike any other you have experienced. This isn't fair and it isn't right. I wish it were different for you and you didn't have to go through it.

The most important thing for you is to be safe. Only you are going to know what you need to do to ensure your safety. You also need to make sure your situation isn't going to drive you to the point of catastrophe, a nervous breakdown, or worse. Take a hard look at your safety, your welfare, and your health, and do what is necessary to maintain these essential aspects.

Sexual harassment - I know this sounds strange, but I know many women who don't know what sexual harassment looks like. My goal here is to discuss the signs and types of sexual harassment so you might be in a better position to recognize it before it gets worse and to make sure you recognize when it has gotten bad enough to do something about it. Unfortunately, I would suggest every woman has experienced sexual harassment of some kind in their lifetime such as being whistled at, casual sexual remarks, or even touching by strangers. And I know women tolerate this to a certain point where it may even be accepted as normal. I don't know any woman who reports being whistled at or when someone says, "Hey good looking" or the guy who happens to brush by you a little too closely. As a result, I think our conditioning of what is acceptable and what isn't may be somewhat tainted. In many organizations, sexual jokes and comments just feel part of the culture, and most women will end up tolerating the behavior rather than doing something about it.

I think this is another form of conditioning. The more we tolerate this mild form of sexual harassment, the more we consider it to be normal. The result of this conditioning can mean you may not clearly see or know when the sexual harassment has escalated. This is the real danger for sure.

Sexual harassment is unwanted, and it can be in the form of sexual jokes, sexist remarks, lewd comments, pin-ups or pornography, suggestive comments, pressure for sexual contact, sexual touching or contact, demands for sexual contact or sex, and sexual assault. I would recommend you pay attention to all forms of sexual harassment and certainly recognize when a person begins to escalate. There are some things you can do personally to prevent sexual harassment, which I will talk about later in this chapter.

Bullying – Similarly, I think it is wise for everyone to know what bullying looks like in order to understand the early signs as well as to know when to act. Bullying can be physical where a person is harmed or their property is damaged. It can also be verbal, where a person is hurt through insults and name-calling. It can be social, where a person is purposely isolated and excluded. And it can be cyber-based, where the use of the Internet and/or social media is used to harm a person.

There are a lot of examples out there of bullying, harassment, and intimidation but here are a few: taunting, being told harsh things like being worthless or ugly, being spit at, being forced to do something you don't want to do, threatening behavior, extortion, stalking, spreading rumors or lies, or having your personal items destroyed or stolen. Again, I would recommend you recognize the first signs of bullying and be aware of what is truly going on. You need to address bullying at the first sign if you can, and most certainly stop the bully as soon as you realize what is going on.

Prevention – If I can do anything, it is help you prevent being harassed in any form it might show up in. And it is possible to prevent it from occurring too. However, there are always those people out there who are determined and will do so no matter what you do, so please recognize these people are the outliers.

Sexual harassment is about showing or exerting power, not sex. However, bullying isn't that simple and a person will bully another for a variety of different reasons, one of which is control.

Harassment is about creating fear, making you feel vulnerable, and controlling the situation or behavior in a way that makes the harasser feel powerful. Given the motivation for harassment, it is often possible to prevent this from happening to you.

Here are some thoughts and ways you can prevent this unwanted behavior from occurring.

Confidence – We talked about this at the beginning of the book, and it is most certainly a key component to preventing harassment from happening to you. If you are confident in your actions and how you speak as a strong individual, harassers may not target you. Harassers are more likely to consider an easy target as a victim.

Communicate – Use your confidence and let people in your working environment know harassment will not be tolerated by you or to others in your presence. The best thing you can do is address harassment as soon as you see it, so if someone makes a lewd remark make sure to ask them to not do it again. This may feel like you are being too sensitive or ruining the workplace vibe, but it will pay off in dividends by preventing harassment from escalating.

Modesty – I'm sorry, ladies, but you need to be careful with how you dress and how you draw attention to yourself to prevent sexual harassment. Granted, it shouldn't matter what you wear as sexual harassment is never your fault. However, in a work environment dressing professionally is really more appropriate anyway. More than anything, I want you to simply understand how you are putting yourself out there, and how this might be interpreted as welcoming advances of a sexual nature. Keep flirting and other sexual behaviors out of the workplace to ensure you aren't unknowingly putting yourself in a potentially questionable situation.

Relationships – If you are uncomfortable around someone for any reason, trust your gut and certainly distance yourself from him or her at work and after hours. Do whatever you can to ensure you are not alone with those you are uncomfortable with. Find co-workers you can trust to develop professional relationships with.

* * * * *

Yes, I have been harassed and bullied in my early years in the workforce. Fortunately, neither resulted in anything physical. Both of my situations were about power.

My stories include a male supervisor who wasn't the brightest guy to work for and who got worse and worse over time. I had a t-shirt I wore to work that had a picture of a mountain range silk-screened across the chest. When I wore it the first time he commented, "Nice mountains" and gave me the eyebrows that went up and down, so I knew he meant my breasts. I wore it a second time and his comment was worse: "I'd like to climb those mountains" followed by a laugh. It wasn't funny to me. In fact, this comment horrified me, and I'm pretty sure the look on my face back to him was worth a thousand words. I never wore the shirt again and told my parents, who suggested since I only had a few weeks left of work, I should just make the best of the situation. I did make the best of it, but he never said another rude or sexual comment again either. Somehow, despite not having said anything, the look of utter disgust I gave him must have been all it took.

A few years later, I had a co-worker who had been working on the same crew much longer than I and was pretty comfortable with his place in life. One day while working in the woods together on a project, he began asking me what my female parts looked like. He said he wanted to visualize them. Once again, I was horrified and used the same look I had before. But this time, I also told him to back off and never ask me this question again. He apologized and never crossed the line again. I reacted in such a way where I shamed him, and he was so embarrassed he could hardly work the rest of the day. Deep down I felt like he was harmless, and it was just his bad manners showing through. But I didn't want to take the chance I was wrong so made sure I was never paired alone with him again.

I was lucky these are the worst stories I have to tell. I have never had to deal with anything beyond this. Sure I've had the distasteful jokes told, a crew of all men who seem to only want to talk about sex, and been called a few overly nice names like "hot chick." To me, these were tolerable and might have come close to my own personal line a few times, but never crossed it. For other women, these instances may not have been tolerable. Everyone has his or her own personal line. There is nothing wrong with you determining you've had enough or that someone has gone too far. Stand up for yourself and don't let someone cross your line. Not only do you have the right to stand up for yourself, you also have the responsibility to yourself and to other women to as well. And in most cases, you have the law backing you up too.

20

WHEN IT'S THE WOMEN IN THE WORKPLACE WHO ARE A PROBLEM

Unfortunately, it isn't just the men in a man's world that can be challenging. There are the occasional women who can really throw you too. In fact, some women can be worse than any man you've ever had problems with at work. As if we aren't challenged enough as it is, why is it we have people of our own gender who are causing us grief?

The truth is, some women can be as competitive as men. And the even harsher truth is, some women can be more jealous, petty, and mean too. I've often thought women are so much more devious than men ever think of being or even know how to be. The bottom line is, women can be awful too.

If you have crossed paths with a woman who only wants to cause trouble and create drama, you most certainly have a problem on your hands. Even if you didn't ask for it, you are the one who is going to have to deal with it. How you choose to do so will likely follow you for a long time to come and maybe even your career.

Growing up I never had many friends, which is due to one situation that happened to me in second grade. The start of second grade was great as I was in a class where I began hanging out with a circle of girls, three in particular. I was excited to go to school each day and enjoyed recess time. One day this all changed when this circle of girls turned on me, which was completely out of the blue. I showed up for school and the next thing I knew, this circle of girls was making fun of me, teasing me, asking me to join them and then being abandoned, etc. This was 1976, and if I knew then what I know now, we would have called it bullying. I became a loner and worried every day how I was going to survive being tormented. These girls turned on me, and I believe this shaped how I made friends from that day on. I eventually found another group of friends to be with, yet these mean girls remained individuals I had to watch out for until I moved to a different school in seventh grade. I was always watching my back for mean pranks, lies being told, papers being stolen, etc.

What I learned early on is, people like these girls enjoy watching you be miserable, lonely, isolated, and upset. They feed off of this negative energy. It took me until seventh grade to find it in myself to keep bullies and mean girls from creating this feeling inside of me. This is that inner strength I've been talking about. I found mine in seventh grade. It may have been a culmination of many things, but I distinctly remember being bullied by another set of girls and one in particular.

In my new junior high school, it was common for girls to "call out" each other. This meant you were to meet this girl after school and fight. I was terrified the first time I was "called out." I didn't meet the girl after school and ran home instead. I told my parents what had happened and asked what I should do. That night my dad taught me how to fight. He actually wanted me to be good enough at it to be able to hold my own. In fact, I distinctly remember him instructing me to throw the first punch. He told me if I didn't throw the first punch, I might as well not show up at all. And, I was also instructed to throw a first punch that would end it all. I explained the rule at school was that whoever threw the first punch was the one who would go to the principal's office for detention, and the principal would call my parents. My dad said that was fine and handed me a piece of paper with his work phone number on it to give to the principal. He was serious and didn't care if I got in trouble. He wanted it that way as long as I was standing up for myself.

I went to school the next day trying to avoid all confrontation and pretending I had never been "called out" the day before. Yet it was all over school, and I was called a coward. Being called a coward should have humiliated me, but instead it lit a fire in me that I never knew I had. Later in the day, the girl who "called me out" came back around to do it again. She was met with a different person this time. I yelled back at her saying, "If you are going to call me out, we aren't waiting until after school. We are doing it here and now." In the hallway in front of everyone, I threw the first punch at her and she went down. Everyone was shocked, including me.

I landed at the principle's office straight away. The principle had chairs lining the outside of her office where the trouble students sat. Many of them sat there all day, and as everyone walked from class to class in the hallway, these students were on display. I think the idea behind this was to humiliate the students in trouble in front of the entire student body. I was seated in one of those chairs facing the busiest hallway in the school. The principle told me she was going to call my parents. I told her my dad was expecting her call and gave her the sheet of paper he had written his phone number on. She left me sitting there for the next three hours.

Honest to goodness, it was one of my proudest moments. I had thrown the first punch in front of everyone and now I was sitting in a prominent chair where everyone could see me. This wasn't humiliation; this was proving I had gotten in trouble for what I'd done. The element of surprise of throwing the first punch worked and being in trouble was working too.

Turns out, the principle never called my dad—at least not that he ever mentioned. I never told him what happened, so if he already knew about it, he never said.

And the best part was that the bullying and the girls bothering me stopped immediately. I became a different person that day, not a victim. I became my own protector. I walked a little taller from that day forward.

As the story continues, I moved again at the beginning of eighth grade to another town and another school. At my new school, the principal was very friendly to me, which I thought was awfully nice and figured it was his way of making me feel welcome. Then I noticed him everywhere. He was in the hallway between classes near my locker or near the class I was coming from or going to. He seemed to always be within earshot of the lunch table I happened to be sitting at. He was at the bus stop when I got on or off. I finally asked him in a playful and jokingly way if he was following me. He smiled and said, "I just want to make sure everything is working out OK for you and your fellow students." I took that to mean he knew about my first punch and detention at my previous school. My old principle had ratted me out.

I never touched anyone at my new school. I never had to. My newfound confidence and being my own protector had created a different person. I had new tools to handle situations that warranted it. And I learned to use these new tools very effectively. Unfortunately, my new tools included not trusting other girls (and later women as I became an adult), holding back in forming friendships, and being careful not to get too close. Still to this day I only have one best friend and that is my husband, the only person I've allowed myself to fully trust and love. My whole life I have enjoyed other females and have gotten along great with the majority of them, but I have kept them at a distance for the most part. As a result, I never looked or acted like a loner. Yet, I've never had more than a handful of very close friends at any one time over the course of my life. This was my choice and how I protected myself.

Right or wrong, what happened to me was real, and my reaction to it was how I chose to respond. I've never blamed those girls in second grade for me being the way I am. I actually don't find it odd at all that I am the way I am. I don't regret not being the person I could have been. I just am who I am.

I would never tell you that you should be like me as I realize my experience in grade school created a person who has issues with trust and forming relationships. However, I wanted you to have the backstory on how my ability to form relationships with women has shaped me.

In many ways, I think my experience and response gave me a leg up as I entered the workforce and dealt with difficult people. I am very good at being personable and friendly while keeping people at an arms length. This strategy gave me the time to study individuals and determine what was really going on inside. My goal since grade school was to find ways to get along without putting myself at risk, which meant I was willing to try different approaches with people until I could find the right one. Regardless, I sure wasn't immune to certain women who had it out for me. There have been a few.

The main difference I see in myself and other women I have worked with is that I don't try to be personal friends with people at work. My approach is to be kind, generous, friendly, and social. I get to know them personally as well as learn about their family, hobbies, and other interests. But I don't take it to the next level of friendship. I think this is where many women get into problems with their co-workers. I understand occasionally there are going to be good friendships that can result from working relationships, and I don't want to take that away from you. I just want you to be aware of your assumptions going in. Are you one of those people who think everyone is going to be your friend? You want to have great working relationships with strong bonds too, but wanting everyone to be your friend is unrealistic and dangerous. I realize this is easy for me because of my past; I am not a person who needs friends or seeks them out. I am quite comfortable and prefer to have great acquaintances and solid working relationships. You need to evaluate your thought process on this, especially when it comes to mean women at work. Being friends is not the answer.

* * * * *

Why are women mean to each other? In my opinion, I would say 90% of the time women don't get along because they feel threatened or jealous. It isn't always immediately obvious that one of these two things is going on, but if you stand back and give yourself some distance, you will likely find these are the reasons.

Women who feel threatened can feel this way over the slightest of things or big deals. Women in the workplace can feel threatened if the boss seems to have played favorites, or if your idea was selected, or if your project is coming in under budget or ahead of schedule, or even if the dessert you brought to the holiday potluck made everyone rave. Women will naturally dislike the women they feel threatened by. This doesn't mean you shouldn't do your best or try to be more careful so as to not threaten others. You aren't going to know when or what will threaten other women and you shouldn't live your life trying not to. That would be crazy. You just need to understand if there is a problem with a woman at work, it could very well be because she feels threatened in some way.

Women, who we don't think of as being highly competitive, are indeed competitive to a great degree. Don't kid yourself; we women were born to compete with each other just as men do. And our competitiveness is fueled even more by the fact we are so darned self-conscious about ourselves. Women are self-conscious about everything we have and do. We are constantly unsure if we have enough, are enough, etc. And this definitely stems from a lack of self-confidence too. When we question ourselves, question our confidence, and thus question our value, and then see someone else who has it or does it better, the result is a feeling of being threatened.

The parallel issue is jealousy. To me, these are so similar it's hard to separate if a woman dislikes you because they are jealous or feel threatened. I don't know if it matters much, which is why I lumped them together. The simple fact is, if you have something they don't, they are likely to be jealous. If you have the better haircut or the better clothes, there may be jealousy going on. If you seem more at ease talking in front of a large group at work, there may be jealousy there. In addition to being self-conscious, we are always comparing ourselves to others. Do we measure up or not? Sometimes we want more than we have, or are capable of having, or are trying so hard to be someone else other than ourselves. We get caught up in this, and it plays out in our ability to get along with other women.

Women are also very judgmental toward each other. They are judging whether another woman has the right look, is wearing too much make-up, should lose weight, doesn't fit into that dress, etc. The best way to feel better about yourself for many women is to put others down. This is a terrible thing to say, but it is the cold hard truth for many women.

What to do about it is the real question, isn't it? Remember, you aren't going to change this person or persons. The only thing you can do is change your response to them.

If a woman at work dislikes you and is making your life miserable, try to figure out what's really going on. If it is competition and feeling threatened, then respond sensitively to this. Most women are programmed to believe there is scarcity in success. Women believe there can only be one top dog. Most women do not believe there is enough success in this world for everyone, so if they want it, they will fight for it and take it away from you or keep you from getting it. It is sad so many women feel this way, but they do. Maybe you are evolved enough where you don't see it this way, but I guarantee if you are having problems with another woman they sure see it this way.

So your response to her can be to visit with her about your desire to keep her as the top dog. I once worked with an office manager who basically ruled over every detail in that office. I sure as heck didn't want her job, but when she felt threatened by me; I made sure she knew I respected her "top dog" position even though I thought she was clearly overstepping her position and power. I didn't challenge her and played along. She changed from hating me and sabotaging me to falling over backward to help me. It worked like a charm.

Women are often walking around like a peacock spreading their feathers and trying to prove how great they are. You know these women. They are the ones who are always "one-upping" you. If you had a great dinner out with your hubby, she had a better one. If my child did something well, hers did something better. Do you realize how ridiculous it is to play this game? Stop it. With these types of women (which I seem to run across a lot of), I don't even try to talk about myself, my kids, or anything great happening in my life. I make it a practice to only talk about them, compliment them, talk about how great their kids are, etc. And guess what? They eat it up and they take the bait. These women love to talk about themselves and their lives, not yours. And when you show interest in them and ask questions so they can talk even more about themselves, they will think you are the best thing ever. So take yourself out of the equation and focus on them. You will see an immediate and positive response. This takes great self-control to do this and most will think it is not right to have such an unbalanced relationship. But consider this, do you really think you will ever have a healthy relationship with this person? Do you really want one? The answer is no, of course not. So try this strategy and make life easier on yourself.

The most challenging woman I worked with was so threatened by me, she used every chance she had to make me look bad, particularly in front of my peers and supervisor. Because I was able to take a pause and look at the situation from a distance, I could begin to see her coming from a mile away. I saw her game for what it was. If you remember my childhood you know I wasn't going to get emotionally invested in her game and allow her to enjoy that too. Instead, I watched her closely and determined her issue with me was she had to be top dog and was determined to take me out. I knew she was only going to resort to bigger and worse means of taking me out if I didn't try a new approach. No action from me wasn't working. Running home after getting "called out" wasn't the right move, so to speak.

If you can take away the feeling of being threatened, you will resolve a lot of issues with mean women. Mean women seek acceptance and need validation from others. They need and expect others to make them look good and feel good, and if you don't provide that for them, they will get mean. I'm not saying you fall all over these individuals to make them feel good about themselves. I'm just saying pay attention to what is motivating the negative and mean behavior and change your response to it. And I'm not saying you should lie to them to make them feel better either, because that will come back on you and when it does, it will be a much worse situation to deal with than your current one.

Take the time to figure out what is going on behind their behavior. If you do this, you can then try different things in how you respond or interact with people to potentially improve your relationships. Mean women usually have emotional needs not being met; this is the bottom line. And likely, these emotional needs are due to their lack of self-worth or self-value. Everyone has pain in their lives—fears and events that have likely shaped them—and will come with issues and baggage that aren't very becoming. We are human after all: imperfect beings with inabilities to cope properly with some things in our lives. You need to realize that most of the time a person's negative behavior toward you has nothing to do with you at all. You are just who it is being manifested at or toward.

Knowing this, empathy can go a long way toward dealing with someone's behavior. A little empathy, even as hard as it may be to have for someone so horrible, can be the tool you need to understand that this person is doing the best they can with the cards they were dealt.

As with bullying, they may just be seeking control in their lives because they feel they have lost it to someone or something in the past. Maybe they need to be in charge because they need to feel important and need a lot of attention to cope with the lack of self-worth. Maybe, just maybe, they are using something negative they see in you to focus everyone's attention on so others won't see it in themselves.

The fact is, mean women don't honor themselves. They don't know how to, simple as that. You can't change this, nor should you try.

* * * * *

In addition to changing your response to these women, I want you to also do one more thing. I want you to be the woman who has the confidence and self-worth to allow and support other women to be successful first. Yes, you heard me right. First, let yourself be willing to support others and see them succeed. This doesn't mean I want you to cut your own throat or sabotage or limit yourself. This would be disingenuous. Just make it a practice to support the women in your workplace and in your life. It is a heart thing, to be willing in your heart to see others succeed before yourself. It's being able to put aside your jealousy or feelings of being threatened to help others to succeed. In addition to being a heart thing, it's also a karma thing too. I truly believe this.

One of the secrets of successful and powerful people is they genuinely want others to be empowered and successful too. Successful people know how to, and actively seek to, bring out the best in others.

After reading these last few paragraphs, you have likely guessed that the most challenging woman I dealt with in my career was someone who had a primal need to feel important due to her lack of self-worth. Even though we were colleagues, she expected me to treat her as if she was the queen of her domain. I had to find empathy for her within me, which was very difficult because I didn't respect her. I saw how she mowed over her own staff and others. How was I to find empathy for someone I couldn't respect?

Eventually I was able to find barely enough to take some steps forward and to do so in an honest and heartfelt way. I made it known to her how important it was to me to see her succeed, supported her efforts she brought forward, and acknowledged her success in front of our peers and supervisor. This improved the situation greatly, but I had to keep at it on regular intervals or she would rise up again and again. I had to be willing to see her succeed before my success. I had to support her projects before mine. I had to acknowledge her success in front of others before receiving acknowledgment myself.

Did this harm me in any way? No. I wasn't seen as taking a back seat or being second best. She couldn't see it, but my actions of supporting her actually elevated the perception others had of me. I was held in higher regard due to being more inclusive, thinking beyond my own inner circle, and acting as an honorable and professional person. I had created success reaching far and wide, beyond even what my supervisor saw or knew to be true. The people who truly mattered saw it and most importantly, I knew in my heart I had done the right thing.

* * * * *

Be one of these people who can drop the competition long enough to use your empathy for good and to be willing to see others succeed. Regardless of how others treat you, choose to be one of these people. "Treat others as you would like to be treated." Model this behavior and live it fully, and you will be amazed how this comes back to you in turn. Be the woman who supports other women in the workplace. Be the solution. Be the ideal.

21

FAILURE IS NOT THE FINAL FRONTIER

How many of us are afraid to fail? How many of us have failed and were sure the world as we knew it would end? How many have failed and our world did change?

I'm here to tell you, I have made a lot of mistakes in the workplace and I have failed. I won't tell you about all the small or mid-sized failures. I'm going to hit you with the biggest one.

Quite a few years back, serving as the district manager for my district, we were planning a prescribed burn. The prescribed burn was to be conducted by purposely lighting a fire on a landscape to enhance wildlife habitat and habitat for a rare pine tree species. Both objectives needed fire to create the conditions for improvement. Fire plays a natural role in this ecosystem and had not been part of it for decades, which over time had resulted in the creation of undesirable conditions.

After an unusually wet summer with higher than average rainfall, fire managers were allowed to look at a window of opportunity to burn this area. Due to the high elevation of the area and the favorable weather conditions coming into the area following the proposed burn, plans were set in motion to go forward with the burn.

The first day of burning didn't go perfectly, and the burn was stopped to deal with a spot fire just outside of the unit being burned. On the second day, fire managers continued efforts to contain the burn and spot fire. No ignition to add fire to what was already burning occurred. However, a weather event that afternoon changed everything. A cold front came through with unusually strong winds and picked up the fire in the spot and it ran over 6000 acres. What was supposed to be a small burn of less than 200 acres had soon spread across a landscape, burning private land and forcing the evacuation of homes in a small community.

Granted, I didn't light the match that created this, and I didn't make the decision to burn or not burn after the test fire was completed. Yet this happened on my watch and on the district I was responsible for. As a district manager, the district you manage is under your responsibility. And I took this very seriously.

I can't tell you how upset I was driving over the mountain to see what had happened and to meet with fire managers and local law enforcement. Let's just say tears wouldn't stop.

After learning everyone was evacuated safely, a public meeting in the nearby community was planned so the situation could be addressed.

I remember thinking and praying, "Dear God, how am I going to face these people?" All I knew to do was to tell the truth and take full responsibility and I made it clear to all my fire managers that is what we were going to do.

At the public meeting, I stood next to the local sheriff and addressed the public. I had no idea until the next day there were news cameras panned in on my face. Crazy how you can be so focused nothing else matters. I addressed the public, telling everyone what we were doing and why. But the biggest thing I did was stand tall and tell them that if they were searching for someone to blame, it would be me. I told them I took full responsibility for what happened and most importantly, that the "buck stopped with me." I also apologized for having to meet under these conditions and under this situation. And lastly, I apologized to all those who were evacuated.

With the help of a county commissioner moderating the meeting, the sheriff and I took questions. Mostly, I took questions, and I also took a lot of criticism and angry comments. People stood up and yelled at me, cursed at me, called me names, and told me how angry they were. It was a very emotional meeting for me, but somehow with God's grace I was able to hold it together and face the anger. In fact, I have never been under such stress in my job, and I feel I handled the pressure incredibly well with empathy and professionalism.

After the meeting, a teenage girl and her mother I had never met until that moment came up to me. The mother held my hand and told me her daughter was home alone when the evacuation notice came. The mother was at work and had to rush home to get her daughter. Both ladies were scared out of their mind. The daughter had been scared that the fire would burn her over while the mother had worried that she wouldn't get there in time. Then the daughter spoke and said, "I don't blame you. I want to thank you."

I was stunned at these words and said, "Thank me for what?"

The mother replied, "For being honest and sincere." We all hugged, and I told them how much that meant to me.

This was a turning point for me. Yes, many other people yelled and screamed at me that night. But it was that mother and daughter's words that carried me through.

Night came and went. Morning arrived and no homes were lost. In fact, the fire never got close to the homes in the small community that was threatened and evacuated. No one was hurt either. Evacuations were lifted and people returned to their homes.

The front page of most newspapers in the entire state headlined the prescribed burn that had gone wrong. And the lead quote was mine: "I'm sorry we have to meet under conditions like this." The news stories painted a terrible picture of fire managers and me, because that's what sells. One of the television news stations even had a poll on the evening news asking whether I should be fired or not. Suddenly, my name was out there all over the news. People were blogging about me and stories were written about my "inability to manage" and my "poor decision making." "Here's what happens when a woman is moved up the ladder too fast," read one article, and "doesn't know what she is doing," read another. People were demanding I be fired.

The cold front that had produced the horrible wind and fanned the fire into its size had moved past overnight and the rain and cold weather had come behind it. In fact, we even got snow on the fire. In less than twenty-four hours, the raging fire had turned into a wet mess. It was over.

But the public scrutiny was not, and I continued to face the outcry of it all for weeks and months. But here is the interesting thing: many people, particularly the locals, supported both my district fire managers and me. I had one older and very crass local rancher tell me, "You know, I trust you more now than I ever did before." When I asked him why, he said, "Because you told the truth and you took responsibility. If you were willing to do that under this situation, I know you will in the future."

And this sentiment kept coming from many, many others. To say the least, I didn't see this coming. I had more support than I knew what to do with. I was able to take this negative situation and turn it into an opportunity. Fire managers spoke freely about what went wrong, what we learned, and how future efforts would be improved as a result. We never ran from the truth or our responsibility in it. Even though I am not proud of what happened, I am very proud of how fire managers conducted themselves afterward and in the ongoing months ahead.

I have no regrets in how I handled and conducted myself in the aftermath as well. I do not regret telling the truth and I definitely don't regret taking responsibility. And as it turned out, my credibility actually benefited. No one would have guessed that.

I went on to serve as the district manager for many more years after that incident. I didn't have widespread support from everyone. There were still many people who disliked me. It took everything I had to walk, talk, and keep my chin up some days and with certain people. I got better at it each day, yet I would slide backward occasionally.

One afternoon, I was covering the front desk, answering phones and greeting the public. An older man came in and asked if this was the office with the "stupid woman who screwed up and burned up a whole mountain." Most people who first look at me would never guess I was a district manager as I have a young-looking face, plus I was filling in for the receptionist, which you don't see many district managers do. He definitely had no idea, so I stuck my hand out to shake his and said, "Yes, you are speaking to her." Dealing with negative comments from people and handling situations with responses like that became easier and easier for me. But it took time to shake the shame and rebuild the confidence.

I had support from the people who really mattered and this helped as I was rebuilding my confidence. Embedded in this new confidence was the experience of failing and all the emotion that goes with it. I would liken it to a tree that has a nail in it or a piece of wire wrapped around it, yet the tree just grows over and around it. This is what my confidence was doing—growing around it and incorporating it into the person I came to be. The experience changed me to my core and it also made me stronger. I am grateful to know I can do more than just survive through adversity; I can be the person I was meant to be with honesty and integrity. I'm glad to know this about myself and to have learned this because of this experience.

* * * * *

Failure and mistakes really do suck. Sometimes they hurt, create disappointment, create missed opportunities, ruin the day, etc. And generally, it is so hard to see the light at the end of the tunnel or the good in a bad situation. Many of us fear making a mistake, which is even worse because it makes failing seem twice as bad.

Over the years and with my experiences, I have learned a lot about making mistakes and failing, which I will share with you now.

First off, own it – If you screwed up, you need to be the person who can own up to it, admit your mistake, take ownership, and take responsibility. After taking responsibility for the escaped prescribed burn, I had many people tell me how surprised they were, as most people in my position wouldn't do that. Sadly, this is true. Cover-ups and lying never look good on people. We see this all the time play out on the evening news. Don't go there. It won't look good on you either.

Owning it also means you need to be the first to break the news, especially to your boss. This takes guts and confidence, but it is always your best move. Believe me, you never want your boss to hear it from someone else. Someone else may not paint it in the light you would. Someone else could make the story into something much worse than it really is. Besides, if you tell your boss you can then explain what you learned and give assurance it will never happen again.

Be honest and don't make excuses – It is so easy to blame others, technology, etc., and sometimes people will even buy into it. But it isn't honest, and it isn't going to serve you in the long run. Dishonesty and excuses will catch up with you one way or another, guaranteed. You don't want this. It will be much worse the second time around as well.

Learn from your mistakes and determine how to fix it – When your boss or others see you take your mistakes to heart and use them to do better the next time or make improvements, you are showing them you are of strong moral character and a good employee. No one is going to fault you for making a mistake, but they will fault you for making the same mistake twice. Be a leader in how you apply your lessons learned and make improvements. People respond well to sharing stories of failure and learning how you overcame to do better or be better the next time. People relate to this type of learning and will see you as a leader for responding to adversity in this way.

Don't take it personally – I think this was the hardest thing for me to do after the escaped prescribed burn. I took the failure hard and for a while, I took it to mean I was a bad person. I felt like a failure. There is a difference; a mistake means you made a mistake. It doesn't mean you *are* a mistake. When you allow the shame and blame to take over, you lose self-esteem and confidence. This is terrible as this is the time you need self-esteem and confidence the most. Don't make your mistakes turn into self-deprecating thoughts about being a bad person, being someone who doesn't deserve success, or not being worthy enough. This is simply not true. Keep your mistakes and your personal feelings about the kind of person you are separate. This is critical, because if you don't, you will fall into a deep dark hole that is terribly hard to get out of.

Dwelling on the mistake or failure continues to create problems too as it tends to keep people in a downward spiral toward this deep, dark hole. You have to move on. You don't have to do it overnight or at the snap of your fingers, but you do have to move on because you can't change your past. What you can do is create the future of your choosing.

Get over what other people think – This one is hard too. We seek approval from others so often, and after a mistake or failure we worry so profoundly what others will think it almost debilitates us. The fact is, most people will think less of us after we make a mistake. In reality, it doesn't matter what others think because it is your life and not theirs.   They also don't know what you know in your heart to be true. So let them think what they want. Don't give your power away to those who likely don't deserve it. Ultimately, if you can't give up your need to always care about what others think, you are going to lose your ability to succeed.

I love this quote from Michael Jordan when he says, "On 26 occasions I have been entrusted to take the game winning shot, and I missed." Can you image being a star player and failing, especially in front of millions of people, including national or worldwide media? Thankfully, most of us aren't under this level of pressure and scrutiny and neither are our mistakes. Yet it does help put this in perspective.

Failure can be one of life's best lessons and a way of teaching us new things. Failure can result in positive outcomes for you personally if you are willing to be open to what it has to teach you. So take your failures and mistakes, along with your applied lessons and improvements, and take them with you to the top of your career ladder. This is how they are intended to be used, for onwards and upwards!

22

CONCLUSION & FINAL THOUGHTS

It's not easy to wake up each day and make the choice to live like who I think I am and who I want to be. Just like you, I waiver and get down on myself. But the one thing that is certain is that each morning I wake up and try to do it better than I did the day before.

This book isn't meant to cover every issue you run across in the workplace. It would be impossible to do so anyway. You are going to find yourself in all kinds of situations. If you are a woman working outside the home, you will run into issues somewhere down the line. It would be very strange if you didn't.

Because this book can't cover every situation in your working or personal life with regard to gender inequality, take the nuggets and pieces of advice and use them as you are faced with new challenges, new personalities, and new issues at work.

I strongly believe in the idea that you teach others how you wish to be treated. You teach them what you are willing to accept in how you are talked to and treated. You teach them what you are willing to tolerate in their behavior. And you teach them what they can get away with or what you are going to hold them accountable to. More than anything, I think this is the main idea in this book. I've laid out the tools, strategies, and some secrets to dealing with gender inequality issues you will face, but it's up to you to use them, apply them in your own way, and begin to teach others what you are willing to accept or not. And you must be committed to it, or you will show others you aren't serious and it doesn't really matter.

* * * * *

I am here to tell you that you are worthy and you matter in this world. Learning how to be successful in a man's world, or for that matter, this entire world, is possible if you put in the effort. You need to trust yourself and build the confidence in yourself to make it happen. This comes from within, ladies. No one is going to give it to you. You have to create it from within your heart, your soul, and your gut.

Every person on this planet wants to be valued, be heard, and be accepted. This is human nature, and it is one of our basic needs to even survive. As such, you know what others want and what lies beneath their behaviors. And because you know this, it helps you stand back and determine how to best approach the situation. We too, as women in the workplace, want to be valued, be heard, and be accepted. I am of the mind that we shouldn't be willing to live with anything less. Yet we have to make it happen because this isn't going to be handed to us. We have to create this for ourselves.

* * * * *

There is something about a woman who has the confidence, the self-awareness, and the inner strength to be the woman she was meant to be. Do you know what I am talking about? Have you seen it? I don't know what else to call it other than "magnetism." I feel like these women have a manner in which they go about their lives both professionally and personally that has a certain magnetism about it. It's as if everywhere they go and everything they do attracts positive energy.

I see these people attract other positive people. They attract situations that are positive. Their timing is good. They seem to be in the right place at the right time. They seem to know how to capture the moment toward a positive outcome. Have you ever wondered how these people do it? You've probably thought all this time they were charmed or just had good luck.

The truth is, it isn't by coincidence or luck. This magnetism comes from inside, from within their being, and is simply a manifestation of their confidence, self-awareness, and inner strength. You can have this too. It is not reserved for certain people. There isn't a limited supply of this stuff. It is yours to have, but you have to choose it, and if you are like me, you have to wake up and choose it each and every day and throughout the moments of the day. I guarantee, those other women do this too. They struggle with it daily and have to reach for it again and again, especially when in self-doubt or difficult times. There is nothing magical about this; it is simply something you choose to do and to have. It is hot or cold, black and white. You can be a "have" or a "have not."

Lastly, I will leave you with this last piece of advice.

You need to do what is right for you, first and foremost.

You need to be your own champion and take care of what you need for yourself so you can be the woman you were meant to be. You will have many situations and decisions to make in your journey through life where you are faced with what to do. I urge you to make the decisions right for you and for your family. This includes making the smaller decisions along the way leading up to the big ones too. As

I said before, each and every day, or even moment to moment, there are decisions you need to make to do the right thing for you. Choose them wisely and choose them well.

Think about what you will be bringing into practice from this day forward after reading this book. What changes from these new practices will you bring into your life and into the world? I pray you live your days fully—with love, passion, confidence, purposeful consciousness, and inner strength.

Think about the qualities that you want to bring into your life, and allow your life to be blessed because you made it so.

DOWNLOADABLE BONUS CHAPTER
& MORE RESOURCES

Available only to those of you who have purchased this book is a free downloadable bonus chapter titled "**Glass Ceiling Breakthrough**". This includes great information, strategies, and actionable items you can use now in your career to move up the ladder into the position of your dreams. Don't let a glass ceiling get in your way! Learn how to cut through the barriers now. Type in the following link to get your bonus chapter now at:
www.WomanToWomanSolutions.com/bonus-chapter

You can follow Amber's blog at
www.WomanToWomanSolutions.com

To contact Amber for coaching services, please also see the contact page at **www.WomanToWomanSolutions.com**
Or email at **amberkamps1@gmail.com**

ABOUT THE AUTHOR

Amber Kamps has worked for over twenty-five years successfully navigating the career ladder into management and other influential positions. Amber teaches working women how to create their own success with strategies for gender inequality issues, work/life balance, office politics, business communications, and leadership development so they can be more effective in their work with less stress, more confidence, and the inner strength to achieve their goals. Her vision is to help women become who they were meant to be at work and in life. Amber is also a wife, mother of two active teenagers, and a woman who lives life with passion and connection.

To contact Amber or to learn more about products & programs offered, visit **www.WomanToWomanSolutions.com** Or email at **amberkamps1@gmail.com**

Choose to work and live your life strategically with confidence and on purpose.

www.ingramcontent.com/pod-product-compliance
Lightning Source LLC
Chambersburg PA
CBHW070245190526
45169CB00001B/306